BILL BAILEY's
Remarkable Guide
to British Birds

BILL BAILEY's
Remarkable Guide
to British Birds

Written and illustrated by:
Bill Bailey.

Quercus

To my Parents
for instilling in me a love of the Natural World.

Contents

Designed by Joe Magee

Introduction   Viii

Introduction

Once during a walking holiday in the jungles of Indonesia,
I asked an old friend, Victor, who has lived in the tropics
for forty years, if there was anything he missed about
Britain. 'The colours,' he said. 'Everything in the tropics
is exotic, vivid, in your face… I miss the muted shades of
Britain, the autumn, and mostly the delicate, subtle colours
of British birds.'
   It's true, in those latitudes, there is a profusion
of colour, to the point of gaudiness, where the exotic
becomes commonplace. Vic's hankering for drabness stuck
in my mind, and when I got home, I found myself taking
another look at the birds I've grown up watching in my
back garden. Every shade of brown, every heathery hue,
sparked off a renewed appreciation of our own, more dowdy
avian companions.

   And yet...
   The iridescence of a starling, the bright jewel that
is a goldfinch, the tiny flash of electric blue on a
jay's wing. Our native birds still dazzle, albeit in an
understated way. Not as spectacular as a Bird of Paradise
perhaps, but just as beautiful, and a lot easier to see.

   This is my scrapbook, of fifty-one of my favourite
British birds. Most of them are fairly common, some less
so, but they all have something remarkable about them.
   Birds are all around, and the more you discover them,
the more they will entertain and delight you.

       Bill Bailey August 2016

The ARCTIC TERN

This slender and rather beautiful seabird is a migration marvel.

It's smartly attired, with a bright red bill and feet, a black cap atop a slate-grey back, the whole outfit finished off with long tails like trailing streamers. Its delicate appearance is misleading though, as this is an extreme endurance bird capable of a globe-spanning voyage.

Recently, an Arctic tern made the headlines with the longest ever bird migration. A tiny transmitter weighing about the same as a stick of gum was attached to its leg and tracked the entire mindboggling journey from Northumberland to the Antarctic and back. That's a round trip of 59,650 miles. That's more than twice round the planet. It took the best part of a year, so it's not like the BAR-TAILED GODWIT's non-stop marathon (see page 15), but it's still a phenomenal trek.

The Arctic tern is an almost identical twin of the common tern, which also migrates a huge distance, but only to West Africa (West Africa? Pfft, that's nothing compared to the Arctic tern's polar adventure). I say almost identical, because there are some subtle differences. The common tern has an orangey-red beak with a black tip, while the Arctic is pure blood-red, and its tail streamers are slightly longer. They both tend to fly with their heads angled downwards, which marks them out against forward-looking gulls.

The Arctic terns are mostly found in the north of England, Ireland and almost all of Scotland - with large populations on Orkney and Shetland. In fact, I remember being in Scapa Flow one summer, gazing out over this famous shallow bay of the Orkney Isles. Against a blue sky, a flock of Arctic terns was dipping down to the surface of the turquoise sea, the vivid, treeless green of the bay's edge framing the image. I stood on the shingle beach, watching these black-capped sea swallows as they flitted and squabbled, their grating calls bouncing off the gently lapping waves.

As if this scene couldn't be improved, I was then handed a cup of tea and a caramel wafer. I experienced a moment of pure happiness.

BONUS FACT.
When flapping its wings, the Arctic
tern has a faster upstroke, but the
common tern has a faster downstroke.
There you go, that's my first of many
challenges: if you can tell them apart
from that, then you are actually some
kind of wizard.

The BAR-TAILED GODWIT

There are all manner of wading birds with some wonderful names - sandpipers, redshanks, stilts, plovers, knots, turnstones, so why pick the bar-tailed godwit? Why not the golden plover, or even the black-tailed godwit?

Well, it might not look the most exciting of birds, but this hunched, rather drab-looking wader is actually a world-record holder.

In New Zealand in 2007, many of these birds were tagged and tracked by satellite all the way to the Yellow Sea off the east coast of China. The voyage was nearly seven thousand miles - the longest single non-stop migratory flight of any bird. Around seventy thousand bar-tailed godwits make this epic odyssey. This was the just the flock - individual birds made it even further. A female - known rather unromantically by her tag number, E7 - flew non-stop from Alaska to New Zealand, a distance of 7,145 miles, without stopping for food or water for nine days.

This biological phenomenon of a bird can double its body weight before the trip, loading up on worms, crustacea and plants. It then waits for the right conditions and a following wind before taking off with quite unexpected aerobatic skill. Incredibly, bar-tailed godwits sleep on the wing by shutting down one side of their brain. I've tried shutting down one side of my brain during Eurovision, but I still can't fall asleep. And because they're not eating on the trip, they don't need the use of their intestine and some of their vital organs. So the liver, the kidneys and part of the alimentary canal are partially absorbed into their bodies to save weight, then reconstituted once the migration has been completed.

    This act of eating their own
body is known as autophagy or
'autocannibalism' and seems
grotesque, but it gets the job done.
That is extreme flight mode, godwit-
style.
    I've watched them stalking the
mudflats of the Wash estuary during
their winter visits, and it's
sometimes hard to tell them from all
the myriad other wading birds. So
I know what your next question is:
'How do we distinguish the bar-tailed
godwit from the black-tailed godwit,
Bill?' Well, that's an easy one. The
bar-tailed's long bill is slightly
upturned at the end, while the black-
tailed's bill is straight. Glad we
cleared that one up.

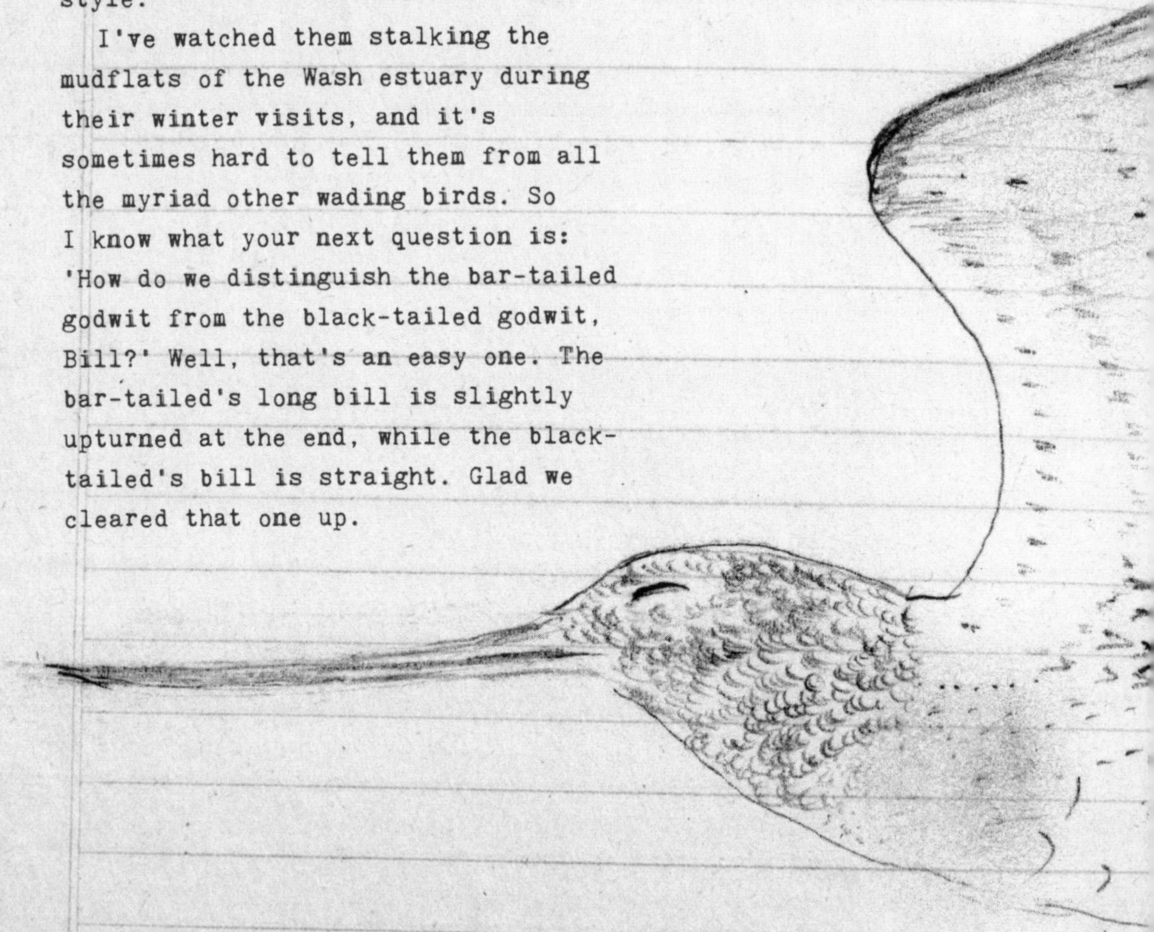

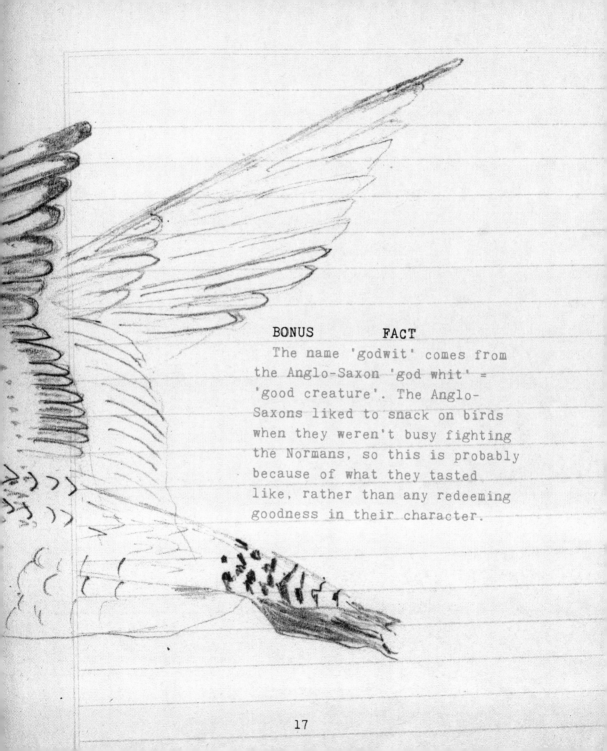

BONUS   FACT

The name 'godwit' comes from
the Anglo-Saxon 'god whit' =
'good creature'. The Anglo-
Saxons liked to snack on birds
when they weren't busy fighting
the Normans, so this is probably
because of what they tasted
like, rather than any redeeming
goodness in their character.

The BARN OWL

The beautiful barn owl is the product of millions of years of evolution.

A perfectly reasonable question might be, where did they live before there were barns?

If you look at some of the other names it's been called over the years - church owl, cave owl, stone owl - you get a few clues.

The barn owl sometimes nests in rocky crevices or hollow trees, but since the advent of farm buildings - or the Barn Age, as I call it - it has found its preferred roosting spot.

I once had a barn owl sit on my head. I was making a TV documentary about barn owls, and I was visiting an owl sanctuary, so under those circumstances, the fact that I was near these nocturnal birds was not that surprising. Barn owls like to perch on wooden posts before hunting, and I was wearing a wooden-post-coloured shirt, so it was fair enough.

I was amazed by how little it weighs for such a powerful hunter. The barn owl's diet consists mainly of voles, but it will also eat frogs, lizards and sometimes other birds. They have superb hearing, and can judge exactly where a vole is in the long grass, and, without even needing to see it, they can pounce in the dark with deadly accuracy. Their ears are not symmetrical, and this allows them to judge distances with great precision. I've also got asymmetrical ears, but I still manage to stub my toe on the kitchen table.

It's a pale and ethereal creature, the barn owl. To see one gliding low over a field at dusk, noiselessly, ghost-like, hunting with its ears, is a sight like no other. The sheer strangeness of its beautiful heart-shaped face, pure white body and silent flight has attracted wonderment and often fear. Which would account for some other names it's gone by - demon owl, ghost owl and death owl . . .

In ancient British folklore, the sound of a barn owl screeching was an omen for imminent death. Which is just superstition, unless you're a vole, in which case it's probably true.

BONUS FACT

The barn owl is one of the most widespread birds in the world, found on every continent except Antarctica. Its average lifespan in the wild is about four years. But one in captivity lived to the age of twenty-five.

The Bill-Vole is in a tight spot.

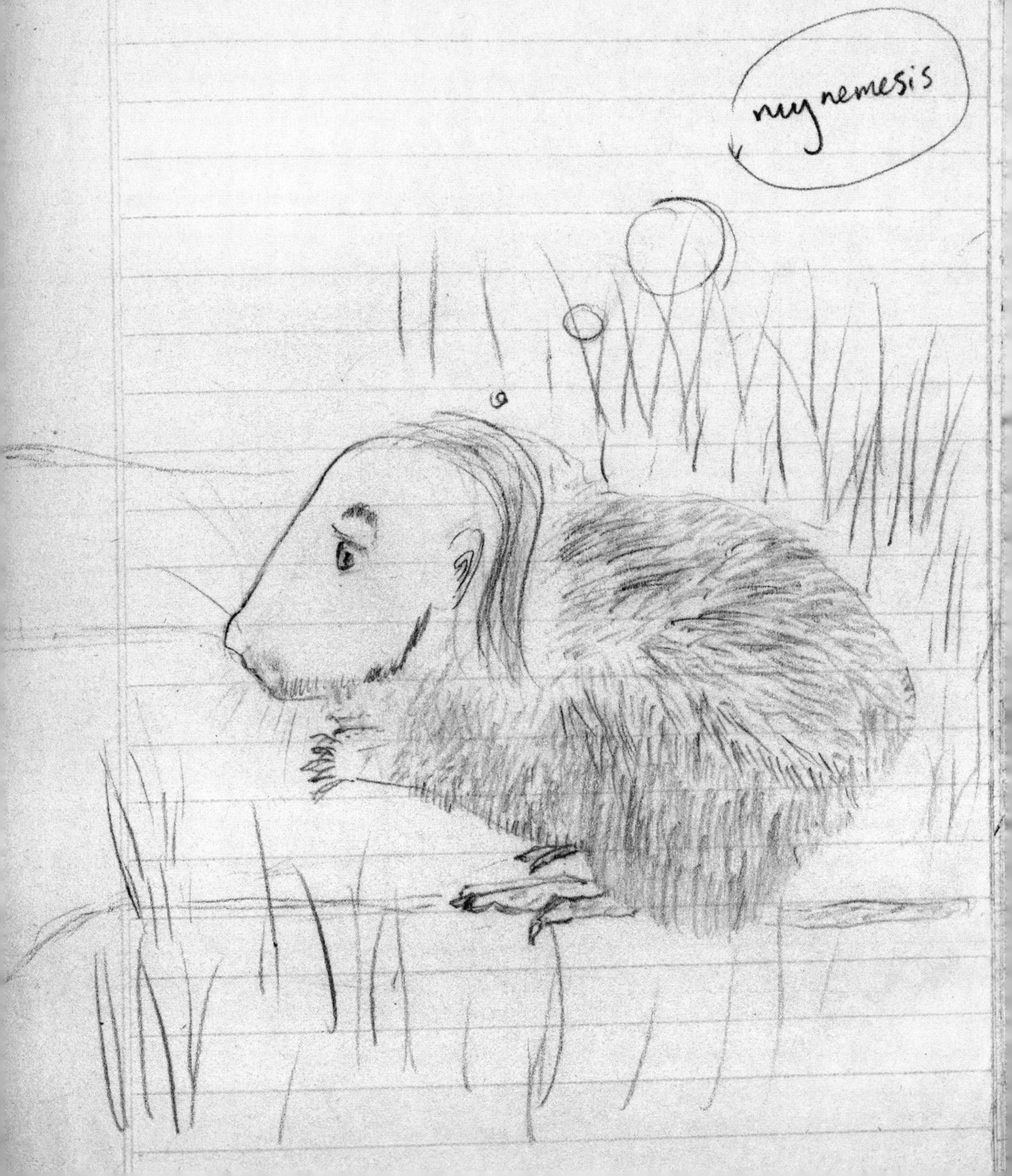
mynemesis

The BARNACLE GOOSE

The barnacle goose's odd name comes from a twelfth-
century myth that this bird actually grew underwater
from a barnacle, then floated off, and somehow flew to
the surface of the water like some feathered mollusc
after the hot summer months. Even though this is just
some made-up nonsense, incredibly, this fantasy lasted
more than five hundred years, and only really died out
in the twentieth century.

The fact is, ancient chroniclers just had no idea
about bird migration. They couldn't explain why the
birds were seen in the winter, and then just seemed to
disappear every summer. Where on earth did they go to
lay their eggs?

Barnacle geese like to raise their young when
temperatures start soaring in the high Arctic of either
Greenland or Svalbard, that far-northerly group of
islands which is part of Norway. In the autumn, they
all begin the long journey to their wintering grounds
on the island of Islay, off the north-west coast
of Scotland, and to parts of Ireland. Their other
favourite hangout is the Solway Firth. I remember
grinning foolishly with delight one holiday there as
a noisy flock of around forty-thousand barnacle geese
whooshed in an arc over my head, and landed in the
field where I stood. This particular colony had just
arrived from Svalbard, apparently, a distance of nearly
1,700 miles. This trek is yet another perverse yet awe-
inspiring feat. Could you make your way from the Arctic

Circle to your house? Just using the stars, the land and
the magnetic field of the earth? With no satnav or gummy
bears for the trip?

   We're only just now beginning to understand the marvel
of bird migration, so I guess we can forgive the fanciful
notions of medieval times.

Bonus Fact

The first recorded instance of this 'goose from a shell' cobblers was from a bloke called Giraldus Cambrensis, who made this unlikely claim in 1186: 'I have seen with my own eyes, more than a thousand of these small birds, hanging … from one piece of timber, enclosed in their shells,' he lied. Why he wrote this, I don't know. Maybe he dreamt it, or perhaps he was a bit of a loner just trying to get a girlfriend: 'Fair lady, these geese, they . . . er . . . they come from barnacles.' . . . 'Wow, I am impressed with your implausible yet amazing goose wisdom.'

Svalbard
1687 miles

The BITTERN

A master of camouflage, the bittern has the cunning habit of craning
its neck vertically and blending in with tall reeds. This shy, secretive
bird is a relative of the heron family, and a rare winter visitor to the

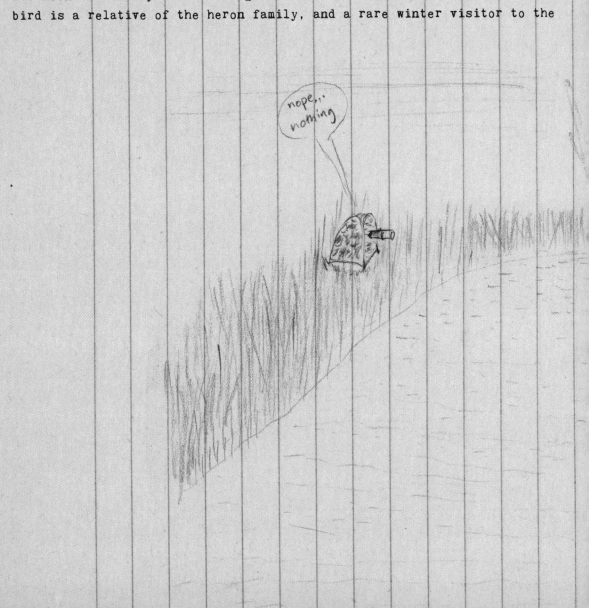

UK. The resident population is small, so it makes this cagey marsh-dweller almost impossible to see.

So good luck with that.

'Yeah, thanks, Bill, include a bird we're never likely to spot. Brilliant.'

OK, I get that, but in this way I'm setting you another
challenge. You'll thank me in the end, you'll see, because it
gives spotting them a real sense of occasion.

I remember a chilly Boxing Day walk around the London Wetland
Centre in Barnes, and finding a huge gaggle of birders in a
state of great excitement. A stretch of boardwalk was bristling
with binoculars, long lenses and spotting scopes. The full
birding paparazzi. All trained on what seemed to be a rather
dull bed of brown reeds. An excited birder grinned at me and
pointing at the reeds, in a stagey whisper hissed, 'Bittern!'
She then offered me the scope. 'Have a look!'

I looked through the eyepiece. All I could see was brown
reeds.

'Amazing, isn't it!' she said, hopping from one foot to the
other with delight. I looked again - more brown reeds. Reedy
and brown. Not bittern-y at all.

'Did you see it?' the birder asked expectantly. I thought,
I can't let her down, so now I'm going to have to pretend that
I've seen it. So, squinting into the scope, I said, 'Wow! Oh,
yeah! … It's amazing how well camoufl--- Wait, what's that?'
Because then, one of the reeds moved and the bittern was
revealed. Like an optical illusion, it had been completely
invisible. No surprise, then, that the collective noun is a
'pretence' of bitterns.

BONUS FACT.

During the mating season, male bitterns make a 'booming'
sound, which can be heard from more than two miles away.
It's a peculiar skill involving filling their windpipe and
exhaling with great force. The muscles around the oesophagus
are developed to create this bizarre and haunting sound.

This gave rise to many of their nicknames: 'bog bumper',
'butterboomer', 'what am I supposed to be looking at?'

OK, not that last one.

The BLACK-HEADED GULL

Not as fierce as a HERRING GULL (see page 94) and
smaller than a LESSER BLACK-BACKED (see page 118), the
black-headed gulls are a graceful sight on our coasts,
inland rivers, and lakes and backyards. It's the most
widespread and familiar of all the gulls.

Here's a bird success story. A hundred years ago,
these gulls were hardly ever seen inland. Perhaps
through a combination of their own adaptable nature,
and a canny eye for the main chance, black-headed gulls
are now the gull species most commonly seen in our
urban and suburban gardens.
Like all the gulls, they are expert fliers and, as
I've discovered, superb catchers of airborne food. I
often cycle down to the Thames with my son, with a
bag of morsels for the black-headed gulls. We fling
them into the air off the riverside path, and marvel
at their aerobatic skills. I think, because of their
smaller size, they're a bit more nimble than the
heavier herring gull. These gulls seem to be able to
hang in the air, pause from a swooping fly-by, and
then immediately adjust their position, almost flying
backwards, if there's a bit of cake in it for them.
If you're feeding them by hand, get your camera phone
ready; they have also a fantastic habit of flying in
close formation, which, if you're lucky, will make for
some excellent action shots.

Feeding these gulls on the Thames, it's reassuring to know I'm continuing a tradition going back over a century. In the severe winter of 1892, the famous ornithologist W. H. Hudson recalled seeing working men on their lunch break heading down to the bridges over the Thames and feeding scraps to these gulls. Some rituals never fade.

The collective noun for these large noisy flocks is a 'screech' or a 'squabble'. Sounds about right.

. BONUS FACT

For hundreds of years, black-headed gulls were seen as a source of food, as their eggs are reputedly very tasty. In 1940, Leadenhall Market in London handled 300,000 of these birds' eggs in a year. The practice of eating gull eggs has all but died out, as the birds and their nests were protected by law as we developed a more enlightened attitude to wildlife generally. But you can still buy black-headed gull eggs. The sale is strictly controlled, and there are only a limited number of licensed egg-traders, but for a hefty price you can try one. I might just stick to hens' eggs though, for my soldiers.

The BLACKBIRD

A familiar sight in our gardens and streets,
blackbirds have adapted very well to living near us,
and often become quite tame.

Male blackbirds stake out their territory in their
first year, which they will keep for the rest of their
lives. Blackbirds are quite solitary birds, and tend
not to have much social interaction. Maybe that's why
they like hanging out with us.

One day a neighbour brought round a tiny blackbird
chick that he'd found on the pavement. It was in a bad
way, and the fact that it was very young made it worse.
It was clear we'd have to nurse it back to strength.

I wouldn't normally recommend hand-rearing an
orphaned bird as it's tricky and the best care it
will get is obviously from its parents. And if the
chick is flightless but fully feathered, mum and dad
are probably nearby, so it's best not to get involved
at all. But in this case, with a tiny, unfeathered
fuzzball with both eyes clamped shut, no sign of the
nest or the parents, we humans were its only hope.
        We named him Pluto.

He was doing well, and we made him a makeshift
portable nursery out of a cardboard box. He needed
constant care, so when I was performing at the Hay
Festival, Pluto had to come too and hang out backstage.
He sadly missed Benedict Cumberbatch - he was too busy
stuffing himself with the mealworms we'd brought along.
When he was old enough, we let him go in the garden,
but he still returns most days, hopping around looking
for a snack. Blackbirds don't tend to travel far from
the nest, and Pluto has got used to the high life. Why
forage around all day, when there's always a free meal
at the Baileys?

BONUS FACT

According to recent research, blackbirds that live in urban areas are affected by artificial light from street lamps and buildings, causing them to breed earlier than those in the country. It's the buzz of the city - it gets to us all.

Lighting-up Times

Day	Lighting Down:	Lighting Up:
Tuesday 1st	05:40	20:11
Wednesday 2nd	05:42	20:09
Thursday 3rd	05:44	20:06
Friday 4th	05:45	20:04
Saturday 5th	05:47	20:02
Sunday 6th	05:49	19:59
Monday 7th	05:51	19:57
Tuesday 8th	05:52	19:55
Wednesday 9th	05:54	19:52
Thursday 10th	05:56	19:50
Friday 11th	05:58	19:47
Saturday 12th	05:59	19:45
Sunday 13th	06:01	19:43
Monday 14th	06:03	19:40
Tuesday 15th	06:04	19:38
Wednesday 16th	06:06	19:36
Thursday 17th	06:08	19:33
Friday 18th	06:09	19:31
Saturday 19th	06:11	19:28

The BLUE TIT

First things first: let's just for a moment deal with
the word 'tit'. Since the nineteenth century, it has been
used as a slang word for breast, but its origins come from
early fourteenth-century usage meaning 'small' or 'a small
creature'. Hope that clears things up.

A common and colourful garden visitor, the blue tit
has a yellow body, greenish back, blue wings and a blue
cap. This may well be the most frequently observed
bird in the country, and certainly one of the easiest
to spot. It is seen all year round, and is particularly
fond of garden feeders in the winter. You'll often
see blue tits accompanied by great tits and coal tits.
You'll hear them too: their call is a mix of whistles,
trills and friendly chirrups.

One of the first birds I ever identified was a blue
tit. I was about six years old, and I liked to hang
out next to the stone bird table in our garden. It
was actually a large cider-press stone, originally
used for squeezing and collecting the juice from
crushed apples. There was a channel around the edge,
designed to collect apple juice, but it was brilliant
fun to fill with water from a bucket, and watch it
flow down the channel to an opening where it cascaded
onto the grass. My mother would scatter scraps and
crumbs, and I loved watching blue tits, among many
other birds, revelling among this buffet of delights,
marooned by my moat.

My other memory of blue tits is of
them pecking the foil off the tops of
milk bottles. When I was growing up in
the 1970s, milk was delivered to our
door in glass bottles with foil tops -
and it was always full-cream milk, none
of that health-conscious semi-skimmed
or skimmed stuff. Back then, there was
no high-speed broadband, so we had to
rely on other forms of entertainment,
like watching blue tits pecking the
foil off the tops of milk bottles. The

cream would rise to the top of
the bottle, which the wily blue
tits somehow knew was a great
nutritional treat. Which is why
many mornings you'd find the foil
pierced through, or even removed
and left in the bushes, folded
into an origami swan. Actually,
that was me.

FOILED.

The BUZZARD

The buzzard is now our commonest bird of prey, a familiar sight soaring by the roadsides. After about 150 years of persecution, the numbers have increased. And even then it's only in the last fifty years or so that they have made a comeback. The introduction of the myxomatosis virus in the 1950s to control the number of wild rabbits had the knock-on effect of decimating the buzzard population. In the space of a couple of years, their main source of food was virtually wiped out. At one stage, it was estimated that 99 per cent of the rabbit population had been destroyed.

Now, you're most likely to see buzzards in the mating season, which runs from February to March, or when the young birds are just finding their wings, from June to August.

If they're not circling overhead at the side of the road, buzzards can be seen where woodland meets open fields, or a bit of moorland. They use thermals - upward currents of warm air, for those of you who didn't listen in Geography - to soar and circle. If you see two buzzards together, it's most likely a pair, with the smaller, lighter male generally rising quicker than the female.

They also like to be near the woods for nesting, and tend to prefer open ground for hunting. Buzzards are large and powerful hunters capable of taking adult rabbits, pigeons, even other birds like crows and coots.

EAGLE

BUZZARD

WREN.

They can hunt in different ways.
I've watched a buzzard on Exmoor sit
for ages on a fencepost just watching,
waiting perhaps for a rabbit, a vole
or even a mole to break cover. Small
mammals, lizards, frogs and often
insects will form a big part of their
diet. As you'll find out later, the
long tail and broad wingspan of the RED
KITE (see page 158) make it awkward for
it to navigate woods, but the buzzard
can hunt among the trees, swerving
and scanning the ground like a hawk.
And sometimes you can see them just
strolling across the ground, looking
for earthworms.

They have a broad and impressive
wingspan, which often leads people to
mistake them for a golden eagle. If
you've seen a golden eagle, you realise
they are a lot bigger. Like a Ford
Focus compared to a Mondeo. This common
error has led the buzzard to have a
nickname: the 'tourist eagle'.

BONUS FACT A flock of buzzards is
known as a 'wake'.

The CANADA GOOSE

The Bill-Goose, during a
localised migration from
sofa to fridge.

The Canada goose might well be the one goose that you are familiar with. You can't miss them, really. Huge, long-necked, black and white honkers, there's usually a mob of them bimbling about in your local park with their big goosey feet. They're not in any hurry. Consequently, they might be the easiest to spot in the whole book. I'm including the largest, the smallest and the fastest of our birds in this book. This might seem a bit harsh, and is by no means an official title, but I'm going to suggest that the Canada goose is Britain's laziest bird.

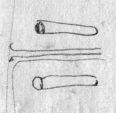

This common resident in our towns and parks was introduced into Britain in the late seventeenth century by King Charles II for his private collection. They were an instant hit among the aristocracy - 'A stripey goose, from Canada, you say? I must have one' - and quickly spread to many other country estates, as the latest fashion accessory.

When the toffs got bored with them and moved on to gazelles or huge lace collars or whatever, the geese escaped, bred and settled in. They were initially seen as unwelcome aliens, but these lethargic waddlers have done exceedingly well here, and have finally been accepted as our own. You'll often see them airborne on one of their localised migrations - except these are more like short excursions - where they fly in a distinctive V-shape formation. This is a wonderful display and sometimes they're low enough for you to hear the air rushing past their wings.

If you find yourself up close to these creatures,
you'll realise just how bulky they are, and in
numbers they can be quite a nuisance. On a rare day
off, I was taking time out for some pitch and putt
on a well-tended and memorable golf course on the
outskirts of Cambridge … or Ipswich … or it might
have been Antwerp. Anyway, a large flock of Canada
geese had chosen it as their hang-out for the day.
After a slightly wayward first shot, I chipped the

ball quite brilliantly on to the first green, and it
seemed to be heading directly for the flag, but at the
last minute it veered off, missing the hole. Arriving
on the green, I was quite revolted by the size and
quantity of the goose droppings. On closer inspection,
I noticed one squidgy green missile in particular that
had been robust enough to throw my golf ball off course
by half a centimetre. Well, that's my excuse, anyway.

BONUS FACTS

This bird's name is misleading. Most of
our population of Canada geese have never
been to Canada, nor have any intention of
ever going to Canada. They will not go to
Canada, unless Justin Bieber takes one home
as part of his entourage. A group of geese
flying in V formation is called a 'skein'.

The CHAFFINCH

The goldfinch might shade it for looks, but the chaffinch deserves a place here not just because it is now one of our commonest birds, but also because it's such a smart and cheerful companion. With the male's neat and colourful rig-out and its lively chattering, it gives off an air of a happy, carefree soul.

A Victorian commentator once wrote, 'to parents with a morose
and sulky boy - my advice is, buy him a chaffinch'. Yes, a
simpler time, when parenting advice was more straightforward.

Many of the birds that used to depend on farmland have
declined in number as farming has become more industrialised
and efficient. No more spilt grain from working horses'
nosebags, and fewer insects due to pesticides.

But the chaffinch seems to have shrugged off these
inconveniences and managed to thrive. So much so, you're as
likely to see one on your garden bird feeder as you are a
country cousin hopping about on a rock in a remote moorland
stream. There are an estimated 7.5 million pairs of chaffinches
in the UK. That's a lot of happy birds.

Its song is a combination of the repetitive and tuneful
- like everything that's good and bad about ringtones. It's
often described as a 'pink pink' call. Or others say it's
more like a 'finch finch' sound, making the chaffinch one

of a select group of animals that can say its
own name. Our pets at home are not capable of
this, although I am convinced I heard our dog
say 'I'm awake' one morning. The chaffinch
actually has two calls: the insistent two-note
repetition, and a longer, more jumbled one,
which is usually a sequence of notes all strung
together, ending with a flourish. It's a bit
like a comedian's sign-off at the end of a set:
'ThankyouladiesandgentlemenI'vebeenachaffinch,
good night.'

Some winter flocks in Britain are all-male,
suggesting that their females have all left them
for warmer climes, only to return and pick up
where they left off. Watching these chaffinches
is the equivalent of seeing blokes shuffle

around, talking about football and eating
takeaways.

BONUS FACT As the above-mentioned Victorian
writer suggested, it was a common custom to
keep a caged chaffinch for its song. Good
singers could reach a price of twenty to fifty
shillings apiece, a huge amount in Victorian
times. Trapping birds was made illegal in 1896.

Lady Lympton's

• CHAFFINCH PIE •

Ingredients:	Some Chaffinches
	Pastry
	Salt.
Method:	Instruct the servants
	to make a Chaffinch Pie.
Serving Suggestion:	In a light heron sauce
	On the terrace
	With a string quartet.

The CORMORANT

I can't think of an unluckier bird than the cormorant (OK, maybe the dodo). Whenever I'm having a bad day, I just think, 'Well, at least I'm not a cormorant.'

Why? Because evolution has played a cruel trick on cormorants. They are waterbirds; they hunt and live in or near water. But while the broad sections of their wings are oiled, the edges are not waterproof.

So when they dive for fish, their feathers become waterlogged and they have to dry them out. It's a familiar sight on the River Thames, a cormorant perched on a wooden piling, its wings hanging out to dry on either side, a weary expression of resignation on its face. Sometimes, I catch the eye of one of them, and the look it gives me always seems to say, 'You think you've got problems.' Although, apparently the 'drip-dry' wing position can stimulate blood flow and help with digestion, so it's not all bad.

I used to live on a houseboat that was called the Cormorant. I think it was meant to imply the boat was an agile master of the water, but, like the cormorant, it was large, black and easily waterlogged. So it was actually a perfect name.

Cormorants are superb underwater swimmers, and can dive down to around eight or nine metres in search of prey. Sadly, their skill has made them the enemy of sport fishermen, and licences have been issued to cull them … for, oh yes, just doing what cormorants do.

I've just seen three cormorants fly in formation across Cardiff Bay, where I am now, while writing this, their short and fast wingbeats a marked contrast to the leisurely gliding of the LESSER BLACK-BACKED GULLS (see page 118). On this occasion, far from feeling sorry for these unfortunates, I am decidedly envious.

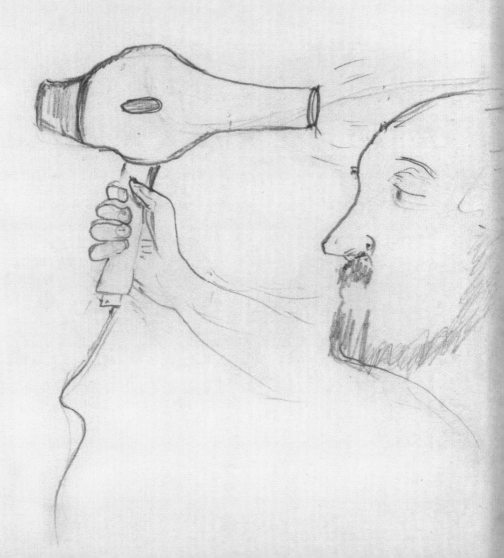

Bonus Fact In China, cormorants are trained to catch fish, but a cord round their necks stops them swallowing the fish for themselves, so they have to regurgitate it up for their human masters. I watched this happen from a wobbly fishing boat on a lake near Dali, in Yunan province. People cheered as the poor snake-necked soggy-winged birds had to cough up their dinner. Like I say, the unluckiest birds.

The CROW

Crows have often been depicted as Harbingers of Evil

This came to me in a
dream, I can only imagine
I must have been eating
cheese late at night.

The crow, or to give it its full name, the carrion crow, is much maligned as a bad omen. Its harsh cawing is the soundtrack of every film and TV historical drama when dark deeds are afoot. It's the ultimate in symbolic portents, shapeshifters, Game of Thrones-type dream sequences - far worse than the BARN OWL (see page 18). Basically, when the crows show up, some sort of grisly death is not far off. The collective noun tells of a history of fear and suspicion: a 'murder' of crows.

Crows have a particularly bad reputation with hill farmers as they have the rather unpleasant habit of bothering pregnant sheep, and attacking them.

All in all, this means they are perhaps among the most unloved of all British birds.

It's a shame, because the crow is actually a rather beautiful bird, its jet-black plumage showing iridescent purples in the sunlight. It's also highly intelligent and communicative.

Once while asleep in a house in Devon I was woken by a tapping sound around 4.30 a.m. Weirdly, I'd been dreaming about being in a house and hearing a tapping sound. The tapping got more insistent. I got up and walked through to the living room, the noise getting louder. And there it was, a crow tapping insistently on the glass door, exactly as if it was saying, 'Look, I don't have my keys, any chance you could let me in?'

I can't help but admire them. They are fighters, and are supremely adaptable. They're tough, street-smart scrappers in the struggle for survival. They've been persecuted for years - hunted, trapped, loathed, demonised - yet now they're seen all over Britain.

The exception to their omnipresence is in the north of Scotland and Northern Ireland, where their cousins, the hooded crows, have staked out their territory. These dapper grey and black birds, known locally as 'hoodies', are a different species. But they've interbred so much that traditionally black crows may well actually be hoodies in disguise.

The way to distinguish a crow from a rook is by its deep black bill. The rook's tends to be smaller and paler. Also, rooks like hanging out in a group, whereas the crow is often seen on its own, or maybe in pairs.

BONUS FACT In an experiment conducted a couple of years ago, crows demonstrated that they could pair up matching picture cards when it led to a food reward.

The DIPPER

A unique and amazing bird, the dipper can dive and swim superbly underwater. Unlike most birds, which have hollow bones, the dipper's leg bones are solid to reduce buoyancy, allowing it to walk along the riverbed underwater and hunt for larvae and small crustacea. They are the weight-belts, if you like, for this scuba diver of the bird world.

Their name comes from their habit of bobbing up and down and cocking their tail while perched.

Because you can only find them in fast-flowing shallow rivers and streams on moorland or uplands, there is a level of difficulty in spotting one (although having said that, the BITTERN [see page 26] still wins hands down in this game). There's an element of adventure in seeing one, as you usually have to be somewhere wild and beautiful. No bad thing. I have climbed over fences, under fences, through fences, over gorse, slithered down banks, got my hair caught on overhanging branches, splashed through icy streams, just to get a glimpse of a dipper. Here's a spotting tip: look out for the telltale white droppings on rocks. Might save you a lot of bother. You're welcome.

    It's when you're in the wilds that you really start
to appreciate how fantastically fine-tuned to their
environment these birds are. I marvel at their ability
to stay underwater for so long, made possible by their
ability to store more oxygen in their blood. Their
sturdy bodies and large powerful claws allow them to
stride against the flow of the water.

I remember walking across the Peak District and seeing
a whole host of different bird species; the one I was most
delighted by was the dipper, and not just because they're so
hard to find. There is something industrious, tough and no-
nonsense about this stout little bird. No flashy colouring,
no showy-offy aerobatics as they fly fast and low across the
water, their wingbeats whirring with speed.

BONUS FACTS

The dipper's eyes have
developed strong focus muscles
allowing them to change the
curvature of the lens to see
better underwater. You might
also like to know that a
population of dippers in Siberia
feeds underwater when the air
temperature is minus fifty-five
degrees centigrade. Now that is
seriously chilly.

The FERAL PIGEON

The feral pigeon is another ubiquitous bird in Britain. It's a good one to begin practising your spotting skills with. No point starting with a spoonbill, or a corncrake, or Richardson's cackling goose (that last one is a real bird before you get all antsy and complain about me making things up).

And when I say 'spotting skills', this might be overdoing it a bit. In the case of pigeons, all you really need to practise is your 'ability to look at things, for example, birds'. They are pretty much everywhere in our cities. They're a major nuisance, and cause a lot of damage and pollution with their droppings. You might have seen little spikes attached to the window ledges of public buildings - well, that's a deterrent, to stop pigeons landing and fouling up the place.

NEST IS LOOKING GOOD
NOTICE TO ABSEILERS CAUTION ANTI-BIRD SPIKES
THESE SPIKES HAVE GIVEN A GREATER RIGIDITY TO THE OVERALL STRUCTURE

These familiar grey and purple-necked birds which
hang around like disaffected teenagers on town
monuments, city squares and in parks really are
'feral'. Pigeons have been kept since as early as 4500
BC, making them the world's first domesticated bird.
Pigeon racing is still a popular sport today, as these
birds possess a remarkable homing instinct. None other
than Charles Darwin was a keen pigeon fancier.

Feral pigeons are domesticated pigeons that have
bred with wild versions, and have themselves gone wild.
They are the streetwise versions of an ancient species,
because all pigeons are themselves descended from the
rock dove, which inhabits cliffs and rocky crevices.
You can see wild populations of rock doves on the
cliffs of Yorkshire. I've seen them at Bempton Cliffs,
and it's here that I got a new-found appreciation for
these unloved creatures. Ferals are superb fliers, one
of our fastest - just take a minute to watch one in
action next time you get the chance. They are amazingly
efficient, powerful masters of the air.

Their huge urban colonies provide further evidence of how
certain species have thrived by being incredibly adaptable.
The wild instinct of the rural birds to live on cliffs is
mirrored in how the city pigeons prefer the high ledges of
urban buildings.

Bonus Fact Pigeons are very intelligent. Research has shown that they seem to know when someone is going to feed them, even appearing to 'recognise' certain individuals who have fed them before.

The GANNET

Watching gannets dive for fish by plummeting out of the sky and arrowing into the water is to witness one of the greatest sights in British wildlife. Once they spot their prey, they tuck their wings in, they turn their bodies into the shape of a jet-fighter, and, gathering velocity, they hurtle towards the water at around 60 mph, exploding beneath the surface like bird-shaped projectiles.

Not only are they physically impressive, they all seem
very bright. Every year in the UK, gannets return in the
summer to the same nesting site, and not just to the vague
bit of cliff they were before. No, to the exact same ledge
they always use. I am amazed by this, and a bit jealous
... I can't remember where I've put my mug of tea down.

Most birds have eyes on the sides of their head, which
has the effect of making them look a bit wary. Gannets'
eyes both face forwards (binocular vision, it's called),
which gives them an intense, almost human expression.
Looking directly at them is unsettling, as I found out
when I was trying to save an injured gannet. It had
probably misjudged a dive and had a damaged wing. It was
not happy about me trying to save it and kept looking
directly into my eyes, jabbing at me with its large and
scary dagger-like bill. Eventually I managed to throw my
jacket over it, and, taking advantage of its confusion,
I wrapped it up and put it in a large plastic box to
take to the vet's.

One of my favourite places in the UK is the islands of
St Kilda off the west coast of Scotland. They are wild and
craggy and beautiful and inaccessible, which only adds to
their appeal, and they're also a haven for seabirds. In
fact, St Kilda hosts one of the largest gannet colonies
in the world . . . over a hundred thousand birds fill the
air, a sight I will never forget.

BONUS FACTS

Gannets are the largest
seabirds in the northern
hemisphere with a wingspan of
over two metres.

Their Latin name, 'morus',
comes from the ancient Greek,
'moros', meaning 'foolish',
referring to how easily they
can be caught. I felt a bit
'moros' myself, after my
nervous struggle with that
injured gannet.

The GOLDCREST

The smallest bird in Britain and indeed in Europe, this exquisite miniature is marginally tinier than the WREN (see page 210). The goldcrest's body is a yellowish grey, but it has this wonderful black and yellow stripe on the top of its head, and in the male this has a bright orange centre.

In the winter, when the resident population is joined by their European neighbours, the numbers can surge up to five million birds. I'm going to make an assumption now: many of you might have never seen a goldcrest. But let me just repeat that figure - there's potentially five million of them! I know they're tiny, but they're out there. Millions of 'em. All over the place! And you can see them all year round.

The best place to look for them is pine forests. But they also pop up in unexpected places.

We were driving on a remote stretch of the A90 between Edinburgh and Aberdeen - it's a picturesque road, with stands of pine on either side that punctuate a rolling countryside. After a stop at a roadside café, instead of the rather uninspiring view of the car park, we ferried our teas to a little side road, parked up on the verge, flipped down the tailgate, broke open the flapjack and - hey presto - instant roadside picnic. Across the road in a stand of bare trees I became aware of movement - tiny flickers of something scooting around the upper canopy. A quick squiz through the binoculars confirmed the spot - a pair of goldcrest happily feeding in this quiet wood. Behind us the traffic droned on - the soundtrack to this scene. People in their droves, whizzing by, oblivious to these delightful birds only a few yards away.

It seemed odd to see what appears to
be such a fragile bird in such northerly
climes, but like their larger cousin, the
wren, they are made of stern stuff, and
resident goldcrest populations have been
found as far north as the Shetland Islands.
They have a habit of perching on fishermen's
nets, earning them the nickname in Scotland
of 'herring spinks'. Although, having said
that, they usually eat spiders, moth eggs
and insects.

BONUS FACT A fully grown goldcrest weighs about as much as a
5p piece. I told you they were small.

CLASH OF THE TITANS

GOLDCREST

vs

WREN

Pine-top face-off

The GOLDFINCH

The goldfinch is a dazzling little gem of a bird, adding a brilliant dash of colour to our backyards. This flamboyant finch is a common visitor to our gardens, and it seems appropriate that the collective noun for a group of goldfinches is a 'charm'.

Its long beak means it can winkle out seeds from thistles and teazles, which are its staple diet. This association with thistles, combined with its red plumage, has led to an association with Christ and the Crucifixion, and the goldfinch has appeared in more than 500 medieval paintings.

They're very sociable and you often find large numbers of them hanging out together by a bird feeder.

I particularly love the goldfinch for its silvery, tinkling song. This was nearly their downfall as, in nineteenth-century Britain, goldfinches - like the CHAFFINCH (see page 50) - were immensely popular as captive songbirds. They were the 'must have' item of the day. Huge numbers were trapped as a result, with as many as 132,000 in 1860 alone. This actually led to the first organisations being formed to protect wild birds, so the goldfinch's song has done all birds a favour.

They are both resident here and migratory. Like British tourists, large numbers of them spend the winter in France or Spain.

In this typical medieval scene,
a huntsman encounters a giant goldfinch.

Leonardo da Vinci wrote of a
superstition surrounding these birds.
When someone was sick, a goldfinch
would be brought in. If the bird looked
directly at the patient, then they would
get well. If the goldfinch turned its
head away, that meant you were a goner.
Who needed doctors back then, when
you had the goldfinch Look of Death?
Unusually for superstition, there's also
a completely opposite interpretation
of goldfinches: that they brought good
fortune. Oh, so not death, then.

There is also an old saying that, if a
goldfinch were to fly over a girl, she'd
marry a millionaire. I can just imagine
a Victorian father flinging a goldfinch
over his daughter's head, and the maiden
saying, 'Papa, isn't this cheating?'

BONUS FACT
Antonio Vivaldi composed
a Flute Concerto in D major
'Il Gardellino', where the
flute imitates the song of the
goldfinch.

The GREAT CRESTED GREBE

A striking and elegant waterbird, the great crested grebe - with its remarkable frondy tufts on either side of its face - can be seen on natural lakes, gravel-pit lakes and reservoirs.

Some of my fondest childhood memories were spent
up at Chew Valley Lake with my family, looking out
for grebes with my grandfather. The great crested
grebe was the prize spot - once we'd seen one, that
meant we could have lunch.

A lovely sight is a female grebe with her chicks
peeking out through her feathers as they take a
ride on her back.

Unfortunately, once upon a time, the ornate
feathers around the crest were used in women's fashion
accessories, like hats, and the soft feathers around
the throat were known as 'grebe fur'. In 1851, a letter
in The Zoologist magazine remarked that the grebe's
feathers were a 'beautiful substitute for furs'. Many a
smart lady about town would be seen in 'grebe-feather'
adornments. Not so lucky for the grebe ...

Unsurprisingly, this led to enormous demand, and
again - you may be seeing a pattern emerge here - these
birds were hunted almost to extinction. By 1860 there
were only forty-two pairs left in Britain.

Laws were passed at the end of the nineteenth century
to protect these birds, and gradually the numbers
went up. Ironically, it was the effects of social and
industrial change in the twentieth century which really
helped the grebe out. The arrival of mass car ownership
and road transport led to huge road-building projects
needing materials like gravel. So artificial lakes
were created by flooded gravel pits, which the grebes
happily moved into.

BONUS FACT: In the mating season,
grebes perform a 'weed dance' where
they approach each other, touch necks
and sway together with large clumps of
pondweed in their beaks. It's
thought to be symbolic of nesting,
and it's one of the most
comically touching rituals
of British birdlife.

The GREEN WOODPECKER

The green woodpecker is the largest of the three
kinds of woodpecker that breed in Britain. It has a
bright red cap, a paler green underwing and a yellow
rump. It nests in a hole in a tree, having pecked the
trunk in the traditional woodpecker style. But unlike
the spotted woodpeckers, it feeds on the ground, having
climbed down effortlessly from its nest thanks to toes
that point backward and forward, allowing it to grip
vertically on to the side of trees.

You'll see green woodpeckers on lawns and in parks
where there is short grass. They use their impressive
bill to dig out their favourite snack: ants. They have
extra long tongues with tiny hooks on the end to snag
their prey.

On a quiet afternoon at the London Wetland Centre
(you'll have worked out by the end of this book that
it's one of my favourite haunts), I watched one of
these individuals digging through the turf for an
ant buffet. I was observing it through my spotting
telescope, because he was quite a way off. This is
where I found out that binoculars will only magnify
so far; sometimes you need the extra reach. If you're
watching birds through a scope, there's a neat trick
where you can hold up a compact digital camera to the
eyepiece of the scope and take a picture. It's called
'digi scoping', but I find this a bit of a fiddle. You
can actually get a good result just with your phone.
Turn on the phone's camera, hold it up to the eyepiece,
and with a steady hand, you can take a pretty decent
photo of the magnified image. It might not win any
awards, but it's handy for identification. And remember
to switch to flight mode.

It has to be said, the green
woodpecker is quite an unusual
bird. It has this curious
undulating flight pattern, with
short bursts of energy, dipping
and gliding, as if the power's
gone one minute, then back with
another upward surge.

It also has a loud, laughing
call which has led to one of
its nicknames, the 'yaffle'.
You can hear green woodpeckers
all year round, yaffling away.

BONUS FACT The green
woodpecker is the bird used in
the Woodpecker Cider logo. I
don't recommend you use this as
a means of identification.

YOU SAID THE
COAST WAS CLEAR!

The GREY HERON

too risky

The grey heron is one of the most adaptable and
successful birds in the country. You're just as likely
to see it in a city park as a remote Scottish loch.
You'll often see them standing motionless by the
water's edge, waiting for the perfect moment to stab at
their prey with a large, dagger-like bill, their long
necks unfurling.

It's the largest predatory wading bird in the country, with the wingspan of a golden eagle. Its stealthy, delicate steps around the water's edge are just as distinctive as its slow, slightly ponderous flight.

Herons build large, messy nests of sticks crammed between the branches of old trees. The male collects all the material for the nest, and the female decides where it goes. Sounds familiar. At some point between February and May, a clutch of four or five eggs will be laid, and once hatched it takes the young herons seven or eight weeks to get their wings. A word of warning - don't get too close to have a look. When herons are spooked they have a habit of vomiting as a defence. Half-digested pieces of eel and a water vole skull on your head is not a good look. Just so you know.

We had a heron problem in our back garden once. It would sneak down on a dawn raid and help itself to the fish in our pond. We tried every defence, but it foiled all of them. It poked its beak through the netting, stepped over the twine and was attracted to the plastic heron that was supposed to repel it . . . So I had this idea I would wait up and, when it arrived at first light, I would scare it off with my son's water pistol. In the best tradition of a stake-out, I got some coffee and doughnuts, filled up the Inundator, or the Ultimate Marinator, or the Aquageddon 500 or whatever it was, and settled in to give our heron friend a soaking. Sadly, I nodded off, and the big thieving git got all our fish. In the end, we bought a plastic crocodile, put that on the pond's edge and it worked a treat. The heron has never returned. Best six quid I've ever spent.

Bonus Fact Despite its diet of fish, eels and the occasional water vole, herons were once much prized at the dinner table. However, the famous ornithologist William Hudson once ate heron and described it as 'a loathsome experience . . . it was tough and had a NASTY TASTE' (his capitals). I am assuming he ate it only once.

NO-MORE-HERONS
£6.00

Heron's snack/danger dilemma

The HERRING GULL

You're sitting on a bench near the seafront on a British seaside summer holiday. A persistent mizzling rain has dampened the appeal of the mini golf course, and

a scolding wind whipping off the incoming tide turns the tips of the grey waves a grubby white. Determined to make the most of this unpromising scenario, you are defiantly holding a bag of chips from the seafront chip-shop. To complete this tableau, a bold and fearsome-looking gull eyes your snack with evil intent, waddling around you as others wheel and cry overhead. This fearless bandit will most likely be a herring gull.

For most of us, when we say seagull, this is the one we are referring to.

Terroriser of the promenade. Dagger-beaked dive-bomber.

Gimlet-eyed snaffler of a million battered sausages.

They are among the most common of all our gulls (there is actually a bird called the common gull, but confusingly it's not that common).

I'm watching a mob of them right now, outside my hotel window on this Hastings seafront. It's low tide and they're all foraging among the exposed foreshore in rock pools, looking for mussels, crabs, or sea urchins. They have a bad reputation as opportunistic scroungers, but they are equally smart and ingenious.

Now they're picking up shellfish, and dropping them onto rocks to crack them open. This is classic seabird behaviour and I can't help thinking that the JACKDAWS (see page 102) have learnt this by watching the gulls.

They're hard birds to love, but I have to respect their brass neck. They are a bloody nuisance, but our coasts and our seaside excursions would be poorer places without them. Birds can't all be songbirds, or pretty garden varieties. They are sometimes raucous scavengers who will nick your last bit of scampi as soon as look at you. But I find myself rooting for these unloved birds. They are intelligent and resourceful and with their pure white napes and grey backs, dare I say, quite handsome. They don't start out this way - the young 'first winter' seagulls have mottled brownish backs, and like juveniles of many species, often look a bit bored and dishevelled.

BONUS FACT

Herring gulls, like other gulls, will often spend long periods just doing apparently nothing. This behaviour has been described as 'loafing'. Well, someone's got to do it.

The HOUSE SPARROW

The house sparrow is one of the most widely spread wild birds in the world.

I've seen this industrious scamp retrieving a chunk of dropped bread from under the table of an outdoor New York restaurant, as well as scratching its ear on a hotel roof in the Southern Alps of New Zealand. I've just reread that sentence, and realised I have done both these things myself.

This is a bird that has really got to travel, grabbed those opportunities, and thrived. Wait, this is me again. Perhaps I was a sparrow in my previous life. That would explain my fondness for crumbs and hopping about in a distracted manner.

In the UK, house sparrow numbers have declined in recent years in urban areas; in fact, it has all but disappeared from London, and these days I rarely see one. It's one of the great unsolved mysteries of British wildlife. Where have all the sparrows gone? There are many possible explanations for this. One is that, in city areas, greenery has been replaced by car parks and other developments. It could be pesticide, sparrowhawks (who, as their name implies, like to eat sparrows) or maybe even radiation from mobile phones. Maybe they just got bored with London, fancied a change. No one knows exactly. Certainly they are not as numerous as they once were.

When it is around, the house sparrow lives quite happily side by side with humans, as its name might suggest. They seem very familiar to many people across the world, maybe because they've cropped up in the literature of many cultures, appearing in ancient texts, hieroglyphs, and even Shakespeare's plays and the Bible. The famous tiny French singer Edith Piaf got her surname from the French nickname for sparrow.

Bonus Fact The Liverpudlian nickname for a sparrow is a
'brown budgie', which brilliantly sums up the domestic pet
nature of its personality.

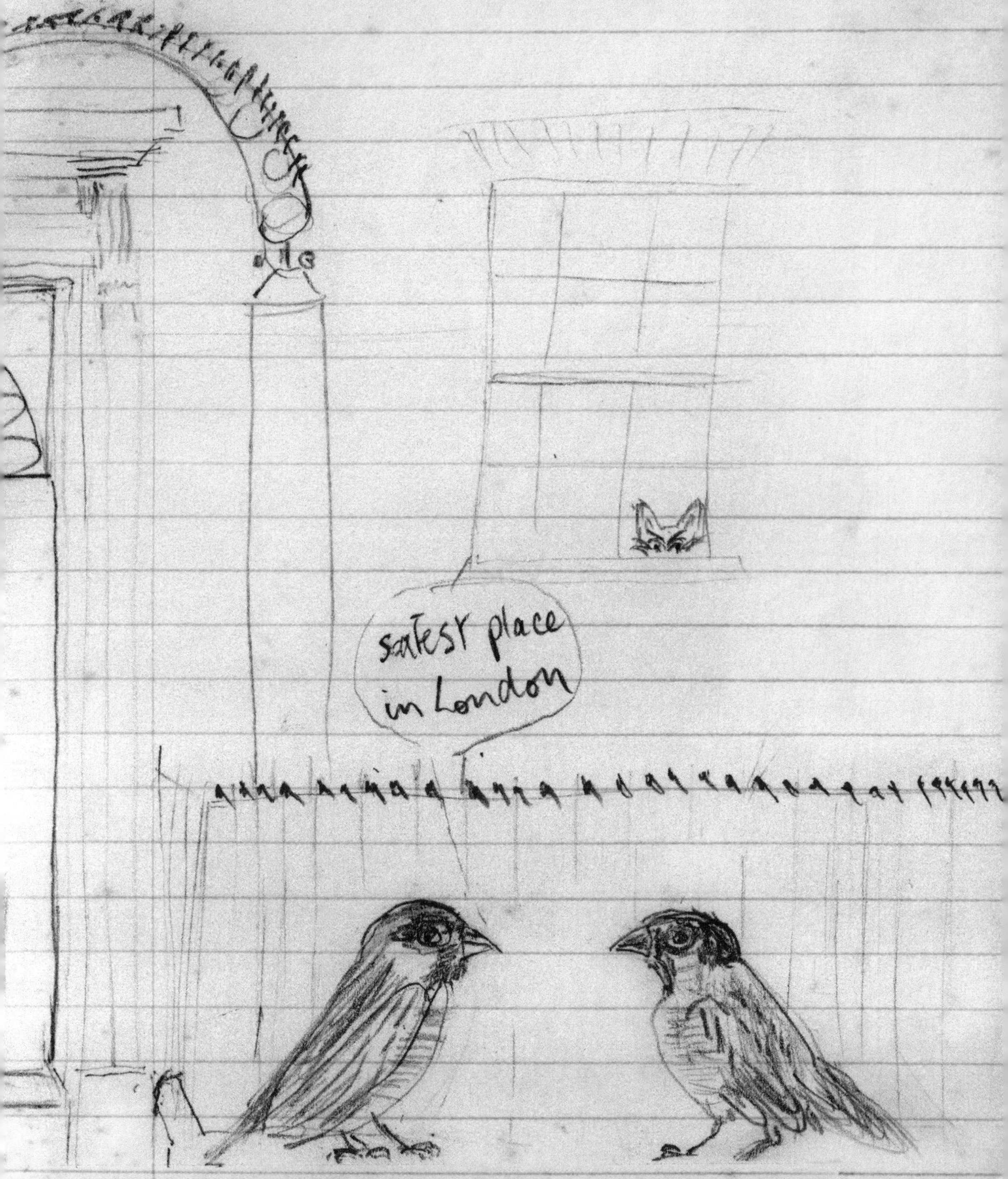
safest place in London

The JACKDAW

The smallest and sassiest of the crow family, these glossy chancers are the jack the lads of the bird world. They are friendlier than CROWS (see page 58), more sociable, and always on the lookout for an easy meal.

They are opportunists, and will live and nest anywhere - sea cliffs, farmland, towns, villages and even your garden if you put up a birdbox. A largish one, mind, such as an owl could fit into.

They stick together, and form strong familial bonds. The same pair of birds will be together for many years, if not for life.

During my stay at a place called The Rookery, I reasonably expected there to be a few rooks. But typical of the way that rooks are always being outdone, it was mainly jackdaws that had moved in. They will nick the food right out from under the beak of a dithering rook. No surprise then that the rooks had moved out.

The jackdaws trundled and scuffled around on the lawn, those beady tykes eyeing me warily. They are also smaller than their corvid cousins, more compact and more handsome in some ways. You can tell them apart by the grey plumage around the head. You can also distinguish them from crows because the adults have a pale white iris around the eye, although this is not so marked in juvenile birds. They have a trademark 'chyak, chyak' call.

I got to see a lot of them in Brighton during the summer. There was a small gang of about half a dozen jackdaws foraging on the shingle beach.

I watched as one picked a
shellfish up in its beak, took
off vertically into the wind,
then dropped it on to the
stones. He did this several
times, swiftly plunging down
with the morsel, never taking
his eye off it, tracking its
fall with precision. After a
few attempts, the shell finally
cracked and he could claim his
prize. A gang of them made
their way steadily up the
beach, hopping and scuttling
along in a companionable way,
for all the world like a bunch
of cocky beachcombers.

BONUS FACT

Jackdaws were once known
as choughs (pronounced
'chuffs'), and in an anti-
vermin statute in 1532,
Henry VIII suggested that
the villages keep baited
nets to catch them, or
face a fine.

The JAY

Your first encounter with a jay will probably consist of just a glimpse of a white rump disappearing into the trees accompanied by a chattering alarm call. Jays are notoriously shy birds, which makes them difficult to spot. If you persevere and get lucky, you'll be rewarded with a wonderful sight, as jays really are beautiful birds.

They are the most lavishly adorned member of the crow family. An overall soft pinkish grey is gloriously offset by a jolt of electric blue on their wing coverts. W. H. Hudson considered them 'not altogether unworthy of being called the British Bird of Paradise'.

They inhabit woodland, and particularly like oak trees in the autumn, when they're on the lookout for acorns. Acorn is glandis in Latin, so this makes up part of the jay's Latin species name, Garrulus glandarius, which means 'talkative acorn eater', 'chattering acorn nibbler' or thereabouts. Its call is quite distinctive and this would account for its Welsh name, Ysgrech y Coed - 'shrieker of the wood'.

They like to bury a store of acorns for future lean times, and, unlike squirrels, are pretty good at finding them again. They will even dig through heavy snow to get at them. Sometimes, though, they're not so good at finding their stash. I'm the same with satsumas. There've been times when I've put one aside in a backpack, 'for later', which meant 'later that day' not two months hence when

I've forgotten about it and the satsuma in question has
turned into a green puffball mushroom. The net result
of the jay's absent-mindedness is that the undisturbed
acorns start to grow, meaning that jays are responsible
for the spread of oak trees. When you're sheltering
under an oak tree next, it might well be the result of
a forgetful jay.

We had a jay nesting in our garden. We deduced this from its constant trips back and forth into and out of the foliage. One afternoon, our cat, Elsie, was poised outside the back door, mid-prowl, chattering in anticipation, when suddenly she took off down the garden. In seconds, she was hurtling back towards me at full tilt, ears flattened, miaowing in fear, being pursued by an angry jay, which was flying low and directly towards me. It pulled up at the last minute, whizzing over my head. Elsie slunk off in a state of shock. Despite the near-miss and subsequent cat-trauma, I never got a finer view of a jay. I won't ever forget the livid blue and the stunning pinkish hue that flashed past my face - a true brush with a garden Bird of Paradise.

BONUS FACT The jay's bright blue feathers are often used in the making of fishing lures.

The KESTREL

Even though BUZZARDS (see page 42) have overtaken
them as our most common bird of prey, kestrels are
often more visible. I have fond memories of my first
kestrel sightings, seemingly suspended in mid-air next
to the M4 on our way to South Wales for the summer
holidays. My father would point them out, and every
time I craned my neck from the back of the car to catch
a glimpse of these aerobatic marvels.

In fact, you will most likely see one near or above
a motorway - its wings a blur, its head motionless
as it hunts for food. They're so numerous in this
particular habitat that they're known as the 'motorway
hawk'.

Motorway verges are actually full of wildlife. Voles
and small mammals inhabit the undisturbed grass there,
which accounts for the kestrel's presence. It's a risky
business, and accidents and collisions are common.
In fact, kestrels are not long-lived birds... never
mind poisoning, shooting or disease, starvation is the
biggest killer. Only one in five birds makes it to more
than two years old. They have to eat up to eight voles
a day. Most British predators, whether they're birds
of prey, mammals or reptiles, eat voles. Voles are
the all-purpose snack, the buttered toast of British
wildlife.

THE MOTORWAY HAWK

For some reason, kestrels don't build their own nests, preferring instead to move into those left by crows or other stick-builders. A hole in a tree will also suffice. No time to make nests, there's voles to catch.

Over the years, the kestrel has acquired the nickname 'windhover', but really it's even more impressive than that. Rather than hovering, it's actually flying slightly forwards, then allowing itself to be blown back by the wind. This requires precision flying and superb coordination as it compensates for this slight backward motion by stretching its neck imperceptibly forward. The head never moves more than six millimetres in any direction and the whole manoeuvre takes less than a second. Next time you glimpse a 'hovering' kestrel from the back of a car, take a minute to marvel at the physics, the power, and the sheer beauty of this roadside air show.

BONUS FACTS When a farmer is cutting his grass or ploughing a field, kestrels will often sit on a post, watching, as if they know that wildlife will be disturbed and thus revealed.

They have superb eyesight and can track and catch a beetle from 50 metres.

The KINGFISHER

You may have never seen a kingfisher. Which is understandable, as they are one of the hardest birds to spot. But don't give up - catching sight of one is a rare privilege. They are birds with the most dazzling plumage in all these isles, and, like the jay, a glimpse is never forgotten.

In the tropics, I've seen many different versions of kingfishers, which are often fairly common - large gaudy birds of varying degrees of brilliant colour and shape. We have only one type in this country, but consequently it feels all the more special. Its shyness gives it an air of mystique, I think, and its magical iridescence is a reward for a lucky spot.

I had such an experience recently. It was a complete delight, especially as it happened as the result of one of my favourite extracurricular activities: stand-up paddle-boarding. I was paddling down the River Brent with a friend on a summer's evening. The plan was to start in Hanwell, then negotiate the locks and river down to the Thames by Kew Bridge.

As we glided serenely under the M4 motorway, where the traffic noise is strangely muted, past a bearded bloke camping under the bridge like a benign troll, there was a sudden flash of movement across the river right in front of me. A blur of bright orange and shimmering azure blue - an implausible amount of colour combined in one tiny whirring ball. To this day, it was one of the greatest birding moments I've ever experienced. The paddle-board helped - the sly way with which it makes progress on the water didn't disturb the bird until I was right on top of it. Normally, I'd be walking or cycling and the bird would have been long gone.

Kingfishers nest in burrows in the river bank, and cleverly angle them at ten degrees so all the droppings can drain away. They are, as the name suggests, adept at fishing, and the record for one pair was 115 fish in one day.

BONUS FACT :
I hate to break it to you, but the kingfisher's feathers are not actually that colourful when examined more closely. Fascinatingly, the colour comes from light striking layers of modified cells in the feather. Their brilliance is magic - it's actually a trick of the light.

The LESSER BLACK-BACKED GULL

Smaller than HERRING GULLS (see page 94), but just as numerous, these equally superb fliers will put on a display of wonderful acrobatic wheeling, complete with mid-air changes of direction and airborne squabbles. Along with BLACK-HEADED GULLS (see page 30), lesser black-backed gulls are among the seabirds you're most likely to encounter, after the herring gull. They are seen all round Britain, mainly on the coast.

In 1956 the government passed the Clean Air Act, which prevented rubbish-tip owners from burning waste. As a result, all the stuff we chucked out every day ended up on tips, or buried in landfill sites. Gulls take full advantage of this chance for a free meal and move in, hanging out around rubbish tips or household bins. Like all our commonest gulls, they are scavengers, pure and simple.

Gulls are understandably seen as the oiks of the bird world, loud and aggressive, jostling for a scrap of discarded chicken kiev on a foul-smelling rubbish tip. But to me, they are also exceptionally beautiful. Particularly on a windy day or when there's a grey, heavy sky, the sight of them in full mastery of the elements is entertaining and actually uplifting. Birds have that habit of raising the spirits. They look at us, cowering indoors, as if to say, 'Well, you might not like it, but we're having fun, wheeeeee!'

They are, at first glance, quite similar to herring gulls, but there are some key differences to help you identify them. Lesser black-backed gulls are slightly smaller, their backs are a bit more black (clue's in the name), while herring gulls are a paler grey. Lastly, and this might be the most obvious variation, lesser black-backs have yellow legs and feet, and herring gulls' legs are pink.

I think it's good to get a handle on identification. You'll
find that usually, for every bird in this book, there will be
several others that look quite similar. What you're seeing,
there, is what the great Victorian naturalists Charles Darwin and
Alfred Russel Wallace saw when they both came up with the theory
of evolution. Small differences in the species are evidence of
change, of one species adapting, evolving, trying to gain a tiny
advantage in the struggle for existence. I find it fascinating
that this is still going on around us, under our noses, as we eat
our chips on the beach and watch them glide and screech overhead.

Bonus Fact It's said that gulls are the spirits of old
fishermen. Old fishermen who liked nicking chips.

The LONG-TAILED TIT

With their comically long tails, and tiny bodies,
these cute fluffballs are sometimes referred to as
'flying teaspoons'. The tails in particular seem way
out of proportion with the body. Mere adornments or
aerodynamic advantage? You decide. It's the Long-Tailed
Tit Tail Dilemma.

I went for a walk once along the Humber estuary, the
huge span of the Humber Bridge providing a striking
backdrop. I was there to look for marsh harriers, of
which there were supposed to be a few, but something
more immediate and noisily interesting caught my
attention: a large flock of long-tailed birds alighted,
fluttering around, totally hyper and excitable, all the
more noticeable thanks to their high-pitch calling of
'tseee tseee'.

They're found throughout Britain and all year round.
I love these birds as they always seem delighted with
the day. 'Woohoo! Over here, check this tree out!
Wow, it's amazing. Wait, what about over here? Yay!'
Moving from bush to tree back to bush in large groups,
calling, chattering, and always active, they are a bit
like kids with a sugar rush. After a brief hangout,
the excitable gang is off again, zipping over a hedge,
their tiny bodies blurring together into a cloud, gone
like a puff of pinkish smoke...

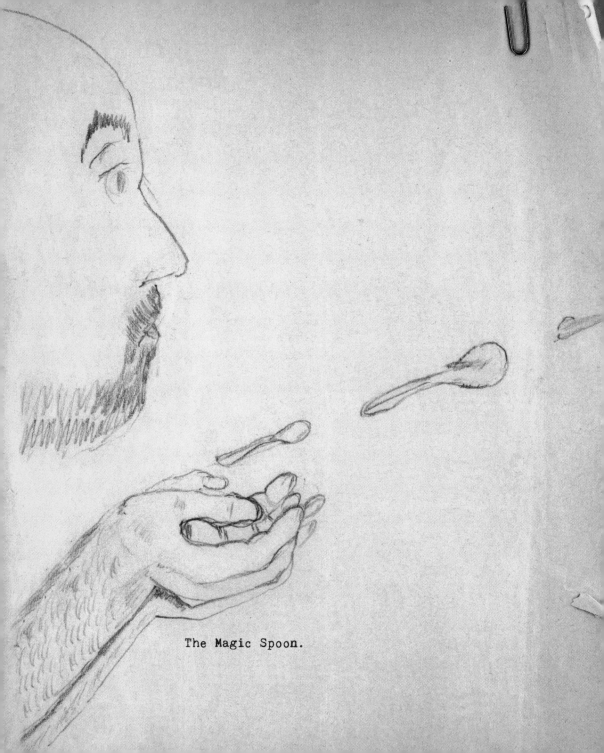

The Magic Spoon.

Not only are they extremely sociable, they are also very supportive of each other when it comes to raising their young. All the other birds pitch in, even if they are parents themselves, or have lost their nests. About two weeks after hatching, the chicks leave the nest, but they all hang out together to look for food.

BONUS FACT Long-tailed tits line their nests with as many as 1,500 feathers, which have either dropped out from their own plumage or are simply stray ones from other birds.

The MAGPIE

There's nothing quite like a magpie. With its
unmistakable black and white plumage and its long tail,
it's a smart bird. Especially when up close, the black
is revealed to have a lustrous purply sheen to it, with
a glorious tinge of green in the tail.

But its dashing looks and inquisitive nature have not earned it many friends. The magpie has a bad reputation, mainly as a thief. It likes shiny things and magpie nests have often been found lined with bits of foil, rings, even car keys. Subsequently, its bold, mischievous demeanour coupled with its physical splendour make the magpie the dandy highwayman of British birds. Its stealing ways are not always so charming, though. It also has a habit of raiding other birds' nests and stealing chicks and eggs.

But there's no doubt that this is a winner in the bird race. Numbers are up, and from having been persecuted in Victorian times, they are now a common sight in our gardens, cities and on busy roads.

When I'm crisscrossing the country on a tour, I am constantly amazed by the sheer recklessness of these birds. Having spotted a bit of roadkill, they hop and fuss about it, pecking away on the hard shoulder of the M6. A couple of feet away - certain death. But the magpies seem to take no notice, blithely skitter-flapping about as three lanes of traffic hurtle by. This is high-risk snacking and sometimes the magpies' luck runs out.

NEW ORLEANS
JAZZ MAGPIE
FUNERAL

But then something amazing happens. Magpies will
sometimes hold 'funerals' for a dead companion. If a
bird is killed on the road, one will start to squawk,
attracting more magpies, and some of them will actually
lay blades of grass next to the body, stand quietly as
if 'paying their respects', then fly off.

The magpie has long been associated with
superstition and bad luck. So much so that I remember
as a child, if you saw a solitary magpie, you had to
hold your collar until you saw a four-legged animal. As
we usually had a dog in the car, this was an easy jinx
to break.

BONUS FACT
It's always good to remember this
traditional rhyme. It's a pretty handy
guide to have.

'One for sorrow, two for joy
Three for a girl, four for a boy
Five for a sandwich, six for a roll
Seven for some crisps tipped out in a
bowl
Eight for marmalade, nine for jam
Ten for some nice piccalilli and ham.'

Ok, it's nearly lunchtime, and my thoughts are getting a
little snack-based.

The MALLARD

The handsome mallard waterbird is our commonest and most widespread duck. In Victorian times, it was known simply as a 'wild duck', as if it were the one and only. The male is more lavishly plumed, with a distinctive glossy green head. The female is brown and plainer, and for this reason I always think the blue and white wing bars are more noticeable on her than on her male counterpart.

Mallards will usually nest in vegetation, near water. You'll come across them in any wetland habitat. The female sits on a clutch of up to twelve eggs for nearly a month, only getting up occasionally to stretch her legs. If a female mallard is disturbed on the nest, she will pretend to be injured to lure away a predator from her eggs, dragging her wings and thrashing about like a demented weasel.

When the ducklings are hatched, often their first journey is over ground, and it's a perilous one at that. The sight of a female duck with a line of tiny ducklings waddling behind is common around our ponds, but it often leads to crossing busy roads. It is a heartwarming picture for us, but it's sometimes a question of life and death for mallards. On top of the risk of getting run over, ducklings that get lost or left behind are often taken by birds of prey, or even killed by other ducks.

One of the many sayings we've got from these birds is 'like water off a duck's back', meaning, 'without being remotely bothered'. It comes from the way that the superbly waterproofed feathers of a duck repel water so efficiently that it is not even absorbed. The liquid forms into tight globules, like

pearls, and simply rolls off their plumage. It's
actually a lovely sight. I never tire of watching this
simple bit of physics, naturally produced and always
quite beautiful.

We found a mallard duckling in the
street outside our house (you'll have
realised by now, there's quite a lot of
bird activity going on where we live).
She'd obviously lagged behind and got
separated from the gang. Amazingly,
she had not been run over or eaten,
so we took her in, naming her
Lucky. After careful nurturing,
and watching her fledge, we built
her a little pond out the back
to hang out in. She lived a
happy duck life for a good
while, until a fox got in one
day when the dogs were out,
and she was gone. I'd like
to think that, because of
her name, she and the fox
struck up an unlikely
friendship, and lived
out their days in a
hedge near the back of
a Nando's. Actually,
I'm pretty sure this
happened.

BONUS FACT Throughout the Middle Ages, mallards were hunted and trapped, often in enormous numbers. The use of a model bird to encourage other ducks to settle on the water became known as a 'decoy' from the Dutch word 'eendekooi', meaning 'duck-cage'.

Wonderful Mallard performance wows the tricky fox crowd.

The OSPREY

The osprey is one of our finest and rarest birds of prey, and, since its tentative return to these shores, it enjoys the highest level of legal protection. As a kid I remember hearing just the idea of ospreys in Britain spoken about as a near impossibility. When you see one, it more than lives up to this mythical status, as it is a magnificent and unique-looking bird. The black stripe over its eye lends it a rakish, villainous demeanour, like some sort of international bird of mystery, which in a way, it is. It is a fishing specialist par excellence and has a spectacular hunting method: once it has spotted its prey, it tucks in its wings and dives at great speed, talons first, grasping the fish and flying off, holding the fish head first to reduce wind resistance.

Like so many other birds, it was nearly extinct last century. Being such an imposing and attractive bird, it was sought by Victorian collectors who, in the fashion of the age, liked to have stuffed ospreys adorning their living rooms. Not content with the bird, there was also a highly lucrative trade in rare birds' eggs. The osprey suffered from this crime more than most, and determined egg-thieves went to absurd lengths to rob their nests.

One of the most successful returns of any British bird, ospreys showed up in Loch Garten in the 1950s. Brilliantly, this became a huge draw, and the centre for observation there has since seen two million visitors.

They are quite common around the world, and I've seen them in the far-flung eastern islands of Indonesia, but seeing them in this country is still a rare thrill.

There was a successful project run by Rutland Water Nature Reserve, near Oakham, and it was there, while I watched them, that I learnt of their yearly trip to their African wintering grounds. Using tagging and satellite tracking, the ospreys' progress was once monitored

as they flew non-stop to the Gambia in West Africa. One particular bird seemed to have stopped off, remaining in a village. Puzzled, a volunteer went along to find out more. Turns out it had been found dead by a local chap, who decided to keep it in his freezer. That explains the lack of movement then.

Bonus Fact In 1851 a notorious egg-burglar called Lewis Dunbar swam out to an osprey nest in a castle in the middle of Loch an Eilein. He stole two eggs, but then, realising he had no bag, tried to swim with one, while carrying the other in his mouth. Nearly drowning, he resorted to swimming to shore on his back, with the eggs on his chest, like some thieving man-otter.

-40°C

The OYSTER CATCHER

If you're near the seashore, there's a good chance you'll
see an oystercatcher. Actually, you may well hear them
first. These stocky and handsome-looking wading birds are
a familiar sight on our coastlines, and announce themselves
with one of the most distinctive calls of British birds.
Their high-pitched, insistent piping call - 'peep-peep-
peep-peep' - is unmistakable, like a flying smoke alarm.

Crisp black and white plumage and a bright orange
bill like a novelty straw make this an ostentatious
fop. Oystercatchers are lovely decorations to an exposed
shoreline, or a mudflat when the tide goes out. Superbly
adapted to the task, they can easily prise limpets off
rocks, which, if you've ever tried to do it, you'll know
will result in scraped fingers or stubbed toes.

Because, you see, it has a misleading name, as it
doesn't actually catch oysters. Well, the British ones
don't, anyway. The continental ones do - after all, as my
mother would say, they are a bit 'à la posh' there.

In the 1970s, cockle fishermen thought (wrongly, as it turned out) that oystercatchers were a threat to their business. So, despite huge public outcry, the government organised a cull. Thousands of birds were needlessly killed, but did cockle numbers go up? Er, no - actually, the cockle numbers continued to go down. More than that, the entire population collapsed. Turns

out the oystercatchers perform a vital
service to the cockle industry, weeding
out the weaker and smaller ones so that
the larger, healthier ones survive,
thus ensuring an overall stronger cockle
species. The government learned a valuable
lesson and vowed never to meddle with
wildlife ever ag--- oh, hang on.

Bonus Fact The oystercatcher can eat about 500
cockles a day, which is nearly half its own bodyweight.
That is a serious seafood habit.

The PEREGRINE FALCON

I know you're not supposed to have favourite birds, but the peregrine falcon might well be mine.

It is a beautiful, agile falcon capable of incredible speed. Just in level flight it can reach 60 mph, which is the diving speed of a gannet, or the maximum speed of my first car, a Citroen 2CV.

But when the peregrine climbs high and spots one of its favourite meals, a pigeon, it then tucks in its wings, adopts what's called the 'stoop' and hurtles into a dive that can reach a speed of a staggering 200 mph. The pigeon doesn't stand a chance.

This perfectly evolved creature is not only the fastest bird in Britain, it's the fastest in the world, and not only that, it's the overall fastest animal species on the planet. It's a missile, the F-4 Phantom jet of the natural world.

Not surprisingly, it's been used for centuries as a hunting bird. The practice of using these birds to hunt - 'falconry', as it's called - began in China four thousand years ago, but it fell out of favour when guns came along and made the whole business of killing game birds like grouse a good deal easier. So peregrines were now the enemy and, like so many birds of prey, were nearly wiped out in the nineteenth century.

Just as they were starting to
return in numbers, the Second World
War came along. Homing pigeons
were taken on RAF bombing
missions so that if the
plane was shot down and the
crew bailed out, the birds
could fly back to base
with details of their
location. They were
deemed essential to
the war effort. Except
what is the favourite food
of the peregrine? Ah. Peregrines
were again the enemy, and in 1940 the
government issued a 'Destruction of
Peregrine Falcon Order'. Around 600
birds were killed, nests and eggs
taken and destroyed. Luckily for the
peregrine (and everyone else), Hitler
was eventually defeated and their
numbers have recovered quickly.

Bonus Fact Falconry is still popular today, although
traditional techniques are being adapted with the advance of
technology. A bait or lure is attached to a drone, which is
then set to hover, encouraging the birds to hunt at higher
altitudes and over a wider range.

Peregrine Falcon 'unimpressed' by wing-suited daredevils

The PIED WAGTAIL

If the KESTREL (see page 110) has adopted motorway verges as its hunting ground, then I would suggest that the pied wagtail has claimed the motorway services.

I've nicknamed them 'car park' wagtails. True, they're seen in all manner of urban environments, from the clipped grass surrounding public buildings, to parks, gardens and golf courses, but I find they're particularly noticeable near Little Chefs, and I am grateful for their companionship on the road. When I'm on tour around the country, I often share a crumb with them on a brief pit-stop at the services, or 'cathedrals of despair', as I call them. During my unremarkable lunch of scalding tea and overpriced panini, their bold and busy presence is a welcome distraction.

The sight of these dapper birds, with their constantly wagging tails and comically fast running, enlivens the dreariest of car parks. I've even seen them strutting along the hard shoulder looking for scraps, and as you know, only magpies are as recklessly daft as that. Perhaps it's because they are insectivores, and have learnt that cars coming off a motorway are often covered in dead bugs. Incidentally, they'll sometimes provide an excellent cleaning service, as they hop on to a car's radiator grille in search of a meal.

I've always found the naming of this and other wagtails confusing. The pied is also known as the white wagtail in Europe, even though its plumage is more grey. Also, there is a different species of bird called the grey wagtail, but this is mainly yellow. And then there's the yellow wagtail, which at least has the good manners to actually be yellow.

Pied wagtails are fond of roosting in winter in large numbers
in towns and cities around Britain. But they also range right
across Europe to Asia, as far as the Bering Sea. I've seen them
cadging crusts from kids on school trips in Helsinki and swiping
baguette morsels from French hikers in the Alps.

BONUS FACT
There is a large pied wagtail roost on Buckingham Palace.
Perhaps they've even cadged biscuit crumbs off the Queen.

The PUFFIN

I love puffins. They're the most unlikely looking
seabirds, more like a child's crayon drawing, with
their gaudy bills and their mournful and slightly
earnest expression. This 'sea parrot' is fascinating
to watch as it 'flies' underwater. On a boat trip
to a group of islands called the Shiants, off the
coast of the Outer Hebrides, I watched a huge raft of
puffins bobbing about in the slack water between tides.
Suddenly they began to take off in their hundreds. It
was a wonderful bit of comic theatre: their stubby
wings working nineteen-to-the-dozen, their serious
faces set in full concentration mode. I sensed a
communal wave of panic seemingly taking over: 'Wooah,
we're not going to make it!' The blur of furious
wingbeats made them look for all the world like huge,
ungainly moths. Add to that the fact its call sounds
more like a West Country 'arr', and it's clear the
puffin is an all-round entertainer.

It's not a rare bird by any means, with around a
million pairs in Britain and Ireland, but nevertheless
it's still under pressure from changes to the
environment. Just a small rise in sea temperature has
reduced the numbers of the puffin's favourite food,
the sand eel. Also like much of British wildlife, it's
facing localised pressures. In one of its strongholds,
the island of Craiglieth off North Berwick, it's under
attack from plants. Not giant sentient triffids beating
the puffins into the sea, but not far off.

The huge and woody tree mallow is so large it chokes
off the puffins' burrows (which they return to year
after year), preventing them from landing and raising
chicks, forcing the birds to abandon their burrows.
I once joined a group of volunteers to prune these
monster puffin-thwarting shrubs in Craiglieth itself. I
remember vividly, on a late summer's day in September,
the precarious landing from an inflatable boat, then
the trudge up the island with my fellow pruners, all of
us armed with shears. The pruning usually takes place
in winter when the puffins are not on land, so a few
stragglers greeted us with anxious calls of 'arr arr',
like a gang of tiny pirates from Somerset.

Things have looked up since the days when these
plump, easily-caught birds were on the menu. On the
remote Atlantic island of St Kilda off the west coast
of Scotland, puffins were trapped in their thousands
and used as a food source, which helped to sustain the
islanders throughout the year. I interviewed a Lord
once and he told me that he was once offered roasted
puffin, but that it had tasted 'absolutely ghastly'.

BONUS FACT: Puffin chicks ('pufflings') are fed in the darkness of a burrow, and never see their parents. Their parents can't see them either. When the chicks emerge, I'm pretty sure neither the parents nor the chicks recognise each other.

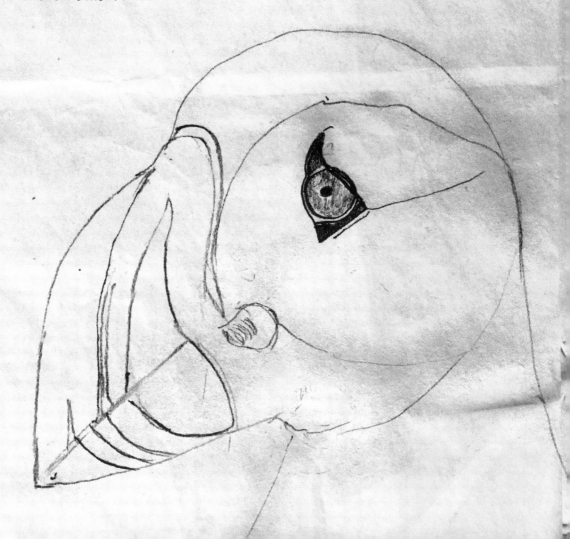

The RAVEN

The raven is the largest member of the crow family - huge, even bigger than a buzzard. These powerful and imposing birds often appear in literature, and are frequently imbued with symbolic power.

As many of you will know, the Tower of London has a resident gang of six tame ravens. There is a legend that if the ravens leave the Tower, then the monarchy will end. That's it, Your Majesty, game over. It's just a superstition, but the guardians of these birds aren't taking any chances. The ravens' flight feathers are clipped so they can't fly off - just in case, Ma'am.

The idea that ravens somehow occupied the Tower of London in the first instance as a symbolic act of keeping the monarchy going is a romantic one, and so persuasive that it has lasted down the centuries. But the real reason for their presence is probably more mundane - and gruesome. The Tower was the location for many executions, and ravens like to feed on dead flesh, so this is what may have attracted them in the first place. No surprise then that a group of ravens is known as an 'unkindness'. A 'revolting unpleasantness' might also work in this case.

Found in upland areas of the south-west of Britain, Wales, the Pennines, the Lakes, and pretty much all of Scotland, these kings of the corvid family mainly eat carrion and small mammals. Their nests are large bowls of sticks and mud, several feet wide, and between three and seven eggs are laid in each one around February time. After the chicks have fledged, these youngsters will stay with their parents at home for six months. Eventually, as adolescents, they will go off and hang around in gangs. What a nightmare for their parents. Although, according to the high levels of stress hormones in a young ravens' droppings, life's tough for a teenage raven.

If you're lucky enough to spot them, ravens are always entertaining. They're more agile than crows, and will often perform aerobatics, seemingly just for sport, occasionally falling or tumbling from the sky into a dive. Sometimes they play with objects, dropping then catching them again in mid-air. They fly in complete loops. One bird was even observed flying upside down for half a mile. Even on the ground they walk with a comical swagger. Their fearsome appearance actually belies a quick mind and a playful intelligence. These are extraordinary, complex and social birds who, through no fault of their own, have come to represent evil. I think the 'unkindness' tag is a bit harsh.

Bonus Fact Ravens are excellent mimics and vocalisers. On a state
visit, the Russian Premier Vladimir Putin was impressed when a raven
at the Tower greeted him with 'Good morning'. It said the same to
Obama - not a fussy bird, politically speaking.

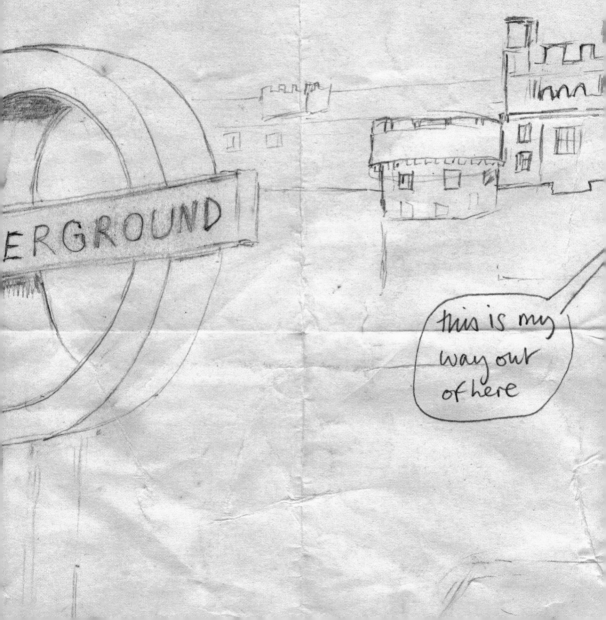

The RED KITE

Red kites were, once upon a time, the refuse collectors, the airborne binmen of the day. So much so, they were a protected species. As we became more civilised in dealing with our waste and rubbish collection the kite's services were not needed. They were driven from the cities, and increasingly seen as a nuisance, a pest even. And when farmers became convinced they were a threat to livestock, well, that was the beginning of centuries of persecution. Since kites are mainly scavengers, feeding on small mammals and sometimes other birds, as well as carrion such as dead sheep, they suffered an unfair reputation as lamb killers.

Hunted to near extinction in the nineteenth century, only a handful remained: by 1903, a species once considered as common as the crow was down to as few as five breeding pairs. In 1989 there was a reintroduction programme around Britain, which has led to well-established kite colonies and around three thousand birds. To witness these magnificent birds of prey once again soaring over the British countryside is a stirring sight, and testament to another great conservation success story.

If you find yourself on the M40 near High Wycombe and at a loose end, look upwards (not if you're driving, obviously). You'll most likely be rewarded with the sight of a red kite soaring on the wind, its forked tail working hard to keep it steady as it scans the ground for its prey. There's something quite romantic about the kite's character. They appear not merely to be hunting for prey; they seem to be revelling in their flight. Buzzards and kites often share their airspace. Buzzards tend to appear purposeful. Kites just seem to like hanging around, twirling and flickering in an effortless aerial ballet.

Bonus Fact Kites have a magpie-
like habit of collecting odds
and ends to decorate their nests:
hats, handkerchiefs, plastic
bags, lottery tickets, even net
curtains. In Roman times it was
reported a kite took hair from
a man's head for its nest. Well,
that's what he said happened.

The RED-THROATED DIVER

A sleek and elegant waterbird, and a welcome summer
visitor to northern haunts, the red-throated diver is a
relative of our other diving birds like the CORMORANT (see
page 54).

The males have this beautiful grey head, with a beady eye
that looks like a stuck on-button, a mottled grey and white
back and the distinctive red-throat of their name. These
colours and adornments look implausibly co-ordinated, more
fashion house than a product of nature. Seeing these birds
is always one of my favourite spots.

These are migratory aquatic birds, seen between April
and October. The winter plumage is quite drab, so lucky
us as we only see them in their summer finery. They can
most easily be seen in the far north of Scotland, so it
required a bit of effort for me to see one, which was a
perk of my tour of the outer islands. It's good to get
a handle on identifying the commonest birds, as this
allows you to practice, and gets you into the habit. But
occasionally you need a mission. And the red-throated
diver was mine. Summer on Shetland is a beautiful place
to be - it has the sweeping treeless green swathes and
sky-blue bays of Orkney, but it is a wilder, starker
landscape. We stopped to take photos, and as always the
binoculars were at hand. I could see a pair of birds
afloat in the calm of a sheltered inlet. They were a
long way off, so I had to use the spotting 'scope but
it was a definite hit. There was the distinctive red
throat and grey neck, bobbing about in one of Shetland's
shallow bays, sunlight roving across the water like a
searchlight through low cloud.

Like the Dipper, it has dense bones to help it
submerge, and even the tarsals in the feet are flattened
to reduce drag through the water. It can dive up to 9
metres in pursuit of a fish.
Like so many waterbirds, they are at risk from oil-
spill, loss of habitat, and fishing nets. Also Arctic
foxes and other large birds like gulls will often steal
their eggs.

Superb in the water, they are quite ungainly on land - their most common nickname is 'loon' which may derive from the old Norse 'lómr', meaning clumsy. I am going out on a limb here and saying they are Britain's clumsiest bird.

BONUS FACT.

Its call is an extraordinary plaintive cry that has become a staple of film soundtracks. It's overused, actually: anytime you see 'lonely' or 'desolate' in a script, you can guarantee a loon call will accompany it in the final edit. These are the atmosphere providers of a thousand wilderness movies. They should be getting royalties.

WooHoo!

The RING-NECKED PARAKEET

The ring-necked parakeet is an Asian parrot, and parrots are not indigenous to this country - mainly because parrots prefer warmer climates and it gets a bit nippy here in the winter. So the first birds here must have been captured or caged birds that escaped and then survived. That first winter must have felt very chilly to them. But the ones who survived were tough cookies. Now they've been here for so long that they are classed as native to the UK.

They are bright green, noisy and boisterous yet have not won many fans here. Notorious trashers of fruit, many bird-lovers dismiss them as unwelcome hooligans. But they are swift and agile flyers, and whatever you think of them, they make a brash and colourful addition to our native birdlife. In India, where they are native birds, they cause enormous amounts of damage to crops, and there are concerns that this might happen here. Their habit of occupying old nest holes in trees could also be a problem for some of our longer-standing native birds. But for now, these raucous green imps are here to stay.

While I was filming the sitcom 'Black Books' in Teddington Studios in west London around 2001, I heard a story about how these birds came to be here. The fanciful tale was that in 1951, some birds were brought over for particular scenes in 'The African Queen', part of which was being filmed at Isleworth Studios, just up the road. Some birds escaped, and this is what led to today's population.

ntral London
mmersmith
4 (A4)

Though there may have been some escapees, it's more
likely that these were from private collections, and
the parakeets have simply increased in numbers over
the years. And they have almost certainly become more
resistant to the cold winters. They have even started
to appear in Scottish cities. In London, a walk around
Richmond Park will undoubtedly feature an encounter
with these fugitives, whatever the season. And at dusk,
driving back along the M4 into London, I have seen
huge flocks of many hundreds of these birds returning
to their roosting sites, a fleeting vision of emerald
plumage, accompanied by raucous flight contact-calling.

Bonus Fact The ring-necked parakeet is the most
northerly parrot on the planet. In just fifty years,
their numbers in Britain have rocketed from zero
to nearly 30,000. Fifty years ago, there were zero
websites being hacked every day. Today, there are
30,000. Just sayin'. I prefer the parakeet's progress.

The ROBIN

The image of a robin in a snowy scene adorns a million Christmas cards, and consequently this plucky pretty creature could make a claim as our most well-known bird. Robins have many collective nouns to describe a group of them, but I think the most appropriate is a 'carol' of robins.

It's a cliché to picture a robin perched on the handle of a garden spade, but like most clichés, it exists because it happens so often. This image really does epitomise its tame and companionable character.

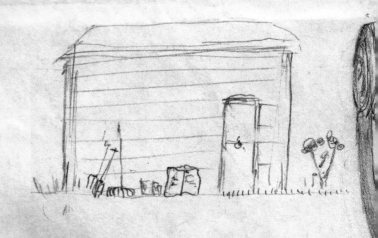

Compared to many common garden birds, the robin's
eyes are larger and darker, and this gives the
impression of it being more 'human'. Because we set
so much store by visual information, this feature has,
I am sure, endeared us to the robin over other garden
birds. In fact, their eyes are proportionally bigger
than ours!

It also appears friendly. It hops around quite
happily when we are out in the garden, apparently
unfazed by human company. Although they are by no means
pushovers. The males are fiercely territorial and will
defend their turf robustly, sometimes quite violently.

Here are two particularities about the robin: first,
they are the only birds that sing consistently through
the winter - while other birds are holing up, these
songsters keep trilling, and the only time they pack it
in for a bit is in summer when they're moulting, and
therefore vulnerable. And second, the robin has a heart
rate of a thousand beats a minute, which is probably
why it appears so perky and inquisitive - hyperactive
even.

Apparently, many small birds have a fast heart
rate, but I reckon it's hard to say for certain. As I
know with our pet bird, Jakob the cockatoo, in order
to check a bird's heart rate you have to restrain it
somehow, which might result in an unnaturally rapid
beat. If I was thinking, 'Aaaagh, I'm in the grip of a
bearded giant,' that would nudge my pulse up a bit too.

BONUS FACTS

Not a fact at all, more of a personal hypothesis, but the popular 1940 song 'A Nightingale Sang in Berkeley Square' describes nightingales singing as 'winter turns to spring'. Well, nightingales are only summer visitors to Britain so there's a good chance the bird they were actually singing about was a robin. That's my theory, anyway. Here's a proper fact: in 1793, the first postmen in Britain wore scarlet tailcoats and were known as 'robins'.

The ROOK

Rooks are very sociable birds, so it's unlikely you'll see one on its own.

At a distance, or seen against the sky in silhouette, it can be quite difficult to tell CROWS (see page 58) and rooks apart. As a general rule, if you see a few crows together, they're probably rooks, and if you see a rook on its own, it's probably a crow … This behavioural difference should mean you are able to distinguish the two.

Around the country, you'll see the evidence of favourite rook nesting spots, with hotels, guest houses and restaurants all called 'The Rookery'. In the eighteenth and nineteenth centuries, a rookery was a term used to describe a slum, a place of rogues and ne'er-do-wells all crammed together in gloomy, tumbledown housing - a clear reference to the untidy and overcrowded nests of rooks, piled one on top of another in ramshackle, noisy colonies.

No surprises that a group of rooks is known as a 'clamour'.

Rooks are very smart birds. In captivity, they have demonstrated the amazing ability to use tools to get food. In one experiment, a floating worm was placed in a glass tube of water, but the level of the water was too low for the rook's beak to reach. The rook used the stones provided and dropped them in the water, raising the level and finally getting their deserved snack. They were also seen to bend pieces of wire to hook an out-of-reach bucket containing a worm to snag the wiggling treat.

Bonus Fact During the breeding season, a male rook will cough up some food from his gullet into the female's mouth. OK, that may seem disgusting, but for a rook couple it's a very tender part of courtship. The human equivalent would be two straws in a milkshake, I reckon.

The SKYLARK

What are the sounds of a British summer? Pop music on the radio wafting from an open car window, as you inch forwards in a queue of traffic on your way to the beach? The haunting combination of panpipes and bongos drifting across a town square? Or just the torrential rain drumming on the roof of a festival tent, while the disposable barbecue hisses in the downpour, its sulky demeanour mocked by the distant crooning of Beyoncé?

For me, there's one sound which sums up an altogether more relaxing and uplifting British summer, and that is the song of the skylark. A song which, although it seems like a disorganised jumble of notes, is performed nevertheless with tremendous gusto, by this small bird rising vertically into

suspicious ploughman
circa 1900.

a clear sky. It's a sound I have enjoyed most summers since childhood. Typically, I'll be lying on my back, somewhere like Exmoor, say, and I'm trying to follow a lark's progress upwards, squinting into the sunlight. Eventually, it climbs too high to be visible, and I give up and close my eyes. Listening to its cascade of notes says lazy days to me.

Its song is its great asset, and that's what earns its place here. Small, brown, a bit mottled, with a sort-of crest on top of its head, the skylark is not the most striking-looking of birds. But until the twentieth century, it wasn't just its fine voice that attracted our attention. Being a bird in the nineteenth century meant your picture would show up in recipe books under 'ingredients'.

It nests on the ground, hidden carefully among the vegetation, and a clutch of three to six eggs is laid in June. Skylark

If I sing I'll drop it.
Can I hum it this time?

numbers have been declining dramatically since the 1990s, mainly
due to changes in farming practices around the country. For many
years, crops were planted in the spring, but now, to make farms
more commercially viable, crops are often planted in the autumn.
The result is that, by April, the crops have grown too high for the
skylark to nest on the ground. This is a real problem, but is being
addressed by farmers leaving small areas with no seeds in their
field, or 'skylark plots'.

BONUS FACT The composer Ralph Vaughan Williams
emulated the skylark's complex and elliptical song
in his beautiful work 'The Lark Ascending'. A group
of larks is known as an 'exaltation', which seems
appropriate when listening to this glorious piece of
music. He took inspiration from a famous poem of the
same name, by George Meredith. Here's an extract:

'He rises and begins to round,
He drops the silver chain of sound
Of many links without a break,
In chirrup, whistle, slur and shake.

For singing till his heaven fills,
'Tis love of earth that he instils,
And ever winging up and up,
Our valley is his golden cup
And he the wine which overflows
To lift us with him as he goes.

Till lost on his aerial rings
In light, and then the fancy sings.'

The STARLING

In autumn, huge numbers of visiting starlings show up in Britain to spend the next few months making the most of our relatively mild winters. When these shivering incomers swell the ranks of our own resident population of starlings, an extraordinary thing happens. At dusk, in their favourite haunts, huge numbers of these birds take to the air, swooshing around in tight formation, before settling for the night.

I have stood and watched this, rapt, my mouth gaping in wonderment at the sight of an immense flock of starlings - sometimes over a million birds - painting huge patterns against the evening sky. The images are constantly morphing into different shapes. One second, a giant hand takes form, then a fish, then a strand of DNA, only to dissolve and fold again in this sentient cloud, this natural art installation.

This phenomenon, known as a 'murmuration', is one of the most spectacular displays in British wildlife, and if you haven't seen it for yourself yet, where have you been? It's not just the starlings deciding to show off, there is a practical reason for this - safety in numbers. A huge swirling mass of birds makes it harder for predators like PEREGRINE FALCONS (see page 142) to focus on one individual.

One of the best known of these flock sites is the old pier on Brighton seafront. I remember one fine evening, after a huge downpour of rain, I was standing on the balcony of my hotel, breathing in the air with that post-rain zing to it. And then, without warning, the sky over the old pier was filled with what seemed to be black smoke. The sound revealed its true nature, this immense fluttering phasing in and out as it bounced off the buildings around. I watched, occasionally laughing out loud with amazement, marvelling at this incredible display.

Starlings are also skilled mimics, and will incorporate the calls of other birds into their song, along with fragments of other sounds like the ringing of a phone, the whooshing of running water, or the creak of a door closing. Their song itself is a jumble of whistles, squeaks, clicks, snatches of melody and sound effects. A bit like scrolling through the frequencies on a radio dial. Mozart bought a starling as a pet in 1784 after he heard one sing a section of his Piano Concerto in G major. His composition 'A Musical Joke', with its seemingly random and abrupt changes and off-key notes, was almost certainly inspired by the song of the starling.

BONUS FACT The name 'starling' comes from the plumage of the juvenile birds which is black and speckled with dots or 'stars'.

A Murmuration of Starlings.

The SWAN

It's huge, serene and quite intimidating. There's really nothing quite like a swan in British birdlife.

There are several species of swan, but the one you're most likely to see is the mute swan. Mute, as in silent. Not an actual mute. A mute is a device you put in a trumpet to dampen the sound and give it a jazzy, 'muted' quality. Don't ever mix these up, as it will end badly. No, it's a mute swan because, quite simply, it has no call.

In fact this is slightly misleading, as the swan is not entirely 'mute'. It's capable of a loud hissing when it's annoyed, and of the odd grunt. Very much like my old Physics teacher, Mr Spalding.

The swan's reputation as unpredictable and sometimes
aggressive is unfounded, although these traits were
well documented with Mr Spalding. There is a myth going
back hundreds of years, as myths tend to do, that if
you get on a swan's nerves it'll basically try and beat
you up, or at least give you a good thwack with its
wings. I remember this information being drummed into
me as a child, rather like the half-life of Radon 214.
So much so, that as a nipper, I was actually a little
bit terrified of these huge white beasts and just
wanted to keep away. Getting kids to be interested in
birds ought to be triggered by enthusiastic cries like,
'Wow! Look at these amazing and totally safe massive
waterbirds!' and not stern warnings such as, 'Don't get
too close, it'll break your arm.'

Actually, they're usually quite harmless (although see Mr Asbo below), and often if they're on a pond in a city park, they'll glide over to accept crumbs quite happily.

For hundreds of years, swans were the property of whoever owned the land they were on. So valuable were they as a meal that their wings were broken so they couldn't fly off, and a little chunk or 'nick' was taken out of their beak to show who was the owner, like clipping a rail ticket. Any swans that didn't have this marker were deemed to be the property of the crown, which meant that all wild swans in Britain belonged to whoever was King or Queen at the time. Pretty smart, these royals. They weren't interested in claiming sparrows or voles, or sphagnum moss. The monarch of the day would be able to approach anyone in the realm and say, 'You there, you at the pond with the bag of crumbs, step away from my swans.' These royal swans were similarly cruelly hobbled, so for about 500 years no one in Britain ever saw a swan fly.

BONUS FACT:

In 2012, an aggressive swan nicknamed 'Mr Asbo' had to be removed from the River Cam in Cambridgeshire. It had been terrorising rowers for several years and was finally caught and transferred to a sanctuary. There's always one idiot that ruins it for the others.

The SWIFT

There's only a brief window in the year to see swifts.
They arrive in April and are gone in August, off on their
long journey back to Africa to spend the winter. But for
those few months, their aerial presence is a welcome sight,
and for me, one that means summer has come to the city.

It's July here in London, and as I look up at around 7
a.m. on this cloudy morning, I can see about half a dozen
of them, high up, their crescent silhouettes darting around
restlessly.

Their short stay here is a busy one, as they have to build
a nest, lay their eggs and raise the chicks in short order.
So material for nest building is gathered on the wing -
feathers, straw, bits of paper - and fashioned into a nest,
often under the eaves of houses or churches, then glued
together with their saliva.

Once the chicks are hatched, they have about six weeks
to prepare for their first flight. This involves a fitness
regime of doing 'press-ups', pushing themselves up on their
wingtips. They have to be ready, because their maiden flight
is not just a wobbly turn once round the block and back
to the nest. It's thousands of miles back to Africa. No
pressure. Imagine being born and your parents saying, 'OK,
you're up on your feet. Great! We're jogging to Madrid.'

When they finally leave the nest and set off with the
other first-time flyers, they will remain airborne constantly
for the first three years of their lives.

They do everything on the wing: eat, sleep, mate … They
are such expert fliers, so why bother with landing?

Another reason for this is that they have very
small and rather weak feet. In fact, there is an
enduring myth that they don't even have feet -
after all, their scientific name is 'apus' which
means 'footless'. They spend nearly their entire
lives on the wing.

On a warm summer's evening, I will often be found sitting outside,
craning my neck back, looking directly up in to the sky, to see
hundreds of swifts burling around, zipping past each other in a
mesmerising aerobatic dance, their calls of 'zeep zeep zeep' leading
to these get-togethers being known as 'social screaming parties'.
Gazing at them at dawn, watching them at dusk . . .

I sound like I'm obsessed. The truth is, I have a huge affection for these birds. I think it's because of my associating them with good times, like an aroma or a favourite pop song - new-mown grass or 'Talk of the Town' by The Pretenders. Their short stay also reminds me of the temporary nature of things, of how we should enjoy and savour these moments.

BONUS FACT Swifts are incredible long-distance fliers - sometimes up to 500 miles in a single day. The oldest recorded swift was seventeen years old, so that's three million miles on the wing. I'd be happy with those airmiles.

The TAWNY OWL

If you hear an owl hooting at night, that will be a tawny
owl. They like to roost during the day, hidden in the foliage
of trees, then fly and hunt at night. They are tricky to
spot, because they are nocturnal, and during the day their
plumage, ranging from red-brown to grey, and speckled with
yellow streaks, makes for excellent camouflage. You might be
lucky and see it being mobbed by small songbirds if they've
discovered its hiding place.

Countless times,
driving back from
a show in the dark,
I have seen them in
a sudden profusion
of mottled brown
colours leisurely
gliding across a
country road.

The male's call is unexpectedly loud, almost
unreal - like a sound effect marked 'hooting owl'.
It consists of one single 'hooooo . . .' then a
more hesitant, fluttering 'woo-hoo-hoo-hooooo'.
The first 'hooo' is almost human-sounding,
which is quite unnerving. It's what is known as
a 'contact call', as it's about letting other
owls, especially females, know where they are.
The female will respond with 'ke'wick' then the
male will hoot back to the female, which also
lets other males know that this is his territory.
Flirting, tawny style.

They mate for life - but make separate nest
holes for themselves, only building a communal
roost when the eggs are about to be laid. Many
human couples might benefit from this arrangement:
stay together, be there for the kids, make some
space for yourselves. I think there's a self-help
guide here. The Tawny Owl Wisdom Compendium -
practical owl-based advice for modern families.

Owls are not the most popular among smaller
birds, as they tend to prey on them, along with
shrews, mice, rabbits, frogs and yes, you've
guessed it, voles. Their hunting method is of the
perch-and-pounce school. But they're quite content
to move into gardens in wooded suburbs, and there,
might make do with a few earthworms or the odd
sparrow.

BONUS FACT Tawny owls don't like flying over water
for some reason, hence they're not found on our islands,
or indeed Ireland.

The WHEATEAR

This smart little bird performs one of the greatest
feats of endurance of any creature on the planet.

Every year, some wheatears migrate from Africa to the
far east of Russia, and some migrate the other way, west to
Alaska, almost meeting up. This second route, the westbound
one, involves a non-stop flight across the Atlantic of
around 2,000 miles. This alone is an extraordinary feat
for a bird that weighs only an ounce, but for the eastbound
population it's a round trip of about 16,000 miles. I don't
know why Siberia holds such an attraction for these birds.
But something compels them to keep flying there. It's one of
the furthest migratory journeys of any bird. And the wheatear
weighs as much as a slice of bread.

If I were a wheatear, I might suggest to the flock,
'Siberia? Again? I hear St Tropez is very nice this time of
year. Anyone?'

They are summer visitors, and can usually be seen between
March and October, and mainly in the north and west of
Britain.

BONUS FACT The name 'wheatear'
comes from the bird's distinctive
white rump. Its origins lie in
Anglo-Saxon times, from 'hvit'
meaning 'white' and 'aers' meaning,
well, 'arse'. In Victorian times,
this was deemed offensive in polite
company, and various convoluted
explanations arose, one being that
it was called after its 'white
ears', lest the vulgar language
cause women to faint.

You can usually spot one on open moorland, and sometimes near
human habitation. Sometimes a few birds appear in the south and
east of the country, and it must have been one of these that I
saw during my appearance on 'Top Gear' as a Star in a Reasonably
Priced Car. I was determined to post a fast lap time, as my first
attempt had been in the wet, and I couldn't find the stick for the

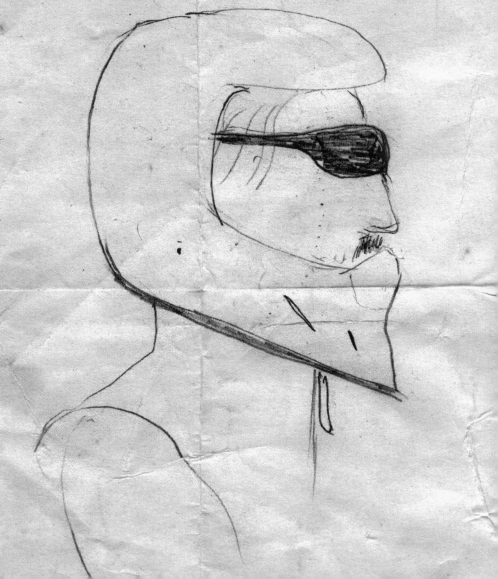

windscreen wipers, so I was all over the shop. I started well, but at the first turn I was totally distracted by a small white-rumped bird scooting away across the grass next to the track. I took my foot off the gas, I looked away from the pile of tyres as I thought, 'Ooh, was that a wheatear? Didn't expect that,' adding precious seconds to an otherwise flawless lap.

Showdown at the Track.

The WHITE-TAILED EAGLE

For me, the white-tailed eagle is one of the most awe-inspiring birds not just of British wildlife, but of the world. The moment I spot one always makes me shiver with excitement. Seeing something so powerful, imperious and so utterly at home in its domain leaves me gasping in wonderment.

It was hunted to extinction in the early 1900s, and the last surviving individual was shot in 1918. A familiar refrain to you now: farmers considered it a danger to livestock. There were even tales of eagles swooping down and carrying off human babies, which seems unlikely, but that particular story persisted down the years. It became such a big part of eagle folklore and so embedded in British cultural life, it received the ultimate mark of acceptance in becoming the name of a pub. In fact, I first became aware of this child-stealing eagle nexus in the Eagle and Child pub in Oxford, a place that used to be frequented by J.R.R. Tolkien, so I was in good company. On the pub sign, a monstrous eagle, presumably a white-tailed, is carrying off an infant wrapped in a shawl. I say presumably because I am not suggesting you should identify birds using pub signs.

The truth is, while it could easily carry off a lamb, the white-tailed eagle's diet tends to be mainly fish and occasionally carrion.

But there is no denying that it is a big and daunting bird. It is the largest British bird of prey, and the largest eagle in Europe. It is truly a magnificent creature, with an enormous yellow beak, huge broad wings with distinctive 'fingers' at the edge, and a prominent white tail - no surprise there, given its name.

After being missing from our skies for nearly seventy years, some young eagles from Norway were reintroduced to the west coast of Scotland in the 1970s. Slowly the numbers have increased and now there are over forty breeding pairs and growing, with a total number of around two hundred birds. OK, it's not a swarm, or a 'convocation' of eagles, as the collective noun has it, but it's progress.

They belong here. This was their hunting ground, and to see them in our skies makes Britain feel a little wilder, like some vital element of our past has been restored.

BONUS FACT. These birds were once common in southern England, with sightings in the 1600s in Norfolk, and in the 1800s as far south as Wimbledon.

Wren on White-Tailed Eagle -->

One-upmanship.

The WOOD PIGEON

The wood pigeon is the commonest pigeon in Britain, larger and more elegant than the smaller urban variety. In fact, it's by far the most prolific wild bird in Britain.

Not everyone is a fan, as their bold presence around the garden feeder can discourage other birds from visiting.

We often see them, or, more accurately, hear them in the cherry-laurel tree in our garden in late winter, feasting on the luscious dark-purple berries.

They are quite bulky birds, and make such a racket clambering about in the branches there's been more than one occasion when I've run out of the house thinking there's a large animal in the tree, that or a clumsy burglar.

They are responsible for a cooing, a murmuring call which is surprisingly powerful and can carry long distances. It's a five-syllable pattern, separated by a slight pause, a comma if you will: 'yoo-hoo, you, woo-hoo'.

I'm looking at my garden right now and, sure enough, I can see a wood pigeon on the lawn. They're remarkably nimble on the ground. When they fly down for a drink, they sip and fly off quite smartly.

One of the reasons for their profusion is their ability to breed all year round. Many birds in this book have a short breeding season, or travel many thousands of miles to raise their young. British wood pigeons tend not to move far from where they're born and raised, and the females will have many clutches of eggs throughout the year.

Rather like their urban FERAL cousins (see page 66), they are not a well-loved bird. Because of their large numbers, and fondness for grain, they cause huge damage to crops. Licences are still being issued to shoot them, although this doesn't appear to affect their dominance. A species that has been around for seven million years, before we were even on the planet, they're another of the winners in the survival game. Supremely adaptable, they are able to co-exist with us quite successfully.

I like their familiar presence, their brilliance in the air. To me, beauty is often in the commonplace. Wood pigeons, or 'woodies' as they are called, are often overlooked as worthy of attention. I guess their ubiquity makes them retreat into the background - they're always there, part of the landscape. But take a minute to appreciate them, and you see a great all-rounder, at home anywhere, living alongside us, a workaday wonder carving up the air in a flurry of metallic green and purple.

And last but by no means least

The WREN

The wren is, on the face of it, quite a nondescript
sort of bird.

It's small, brown and almost spherical, with a short
tail angled straight up, nearly vertical, like a lolly
stick got stuck to its backside.

By small, I mean it's the size of a decent apricot,
or a toddler's balled-up sock. We're talking very
small. Not as small as the goldcrest, but actually
a bit shorter. It's about the size of one and a half
falafels. And while we're on statistics, one mute swan
- you remember, might break your arm, Mr Spalding etc.,
- well, one mute swan weighs the same as 1,400 wrens.
Which is a tug of war I'd love to see.

It has a surprisingly loud singing voice and a
complex song. In fact, in ratio to its size, it has
the loudest voice of any bird in the country. It sings
mainly at dawn, as this is when other males will
challenge him for his territory. These diminutive
crooners will compete for turf in a kind of 'sing-off',
with the females choosing the most captivating song.

It's a proud bird that doesn't like getting upstaged.
When it's angry, its tiny brown body quivers with
annoyance. It prances about tetchily, uttering an
irritated mantra of 'tchik tchik tchik'.

I was trying to spot WHITE-TAILED EAGLES (see page 202) on the Isle of Mull in Scotland one day, as you do, and I heard this disapproving 'tchik tchik' coming from a hedge. It really felt like it had a sarcastic tone, as if the wren was cross with me for favouring the eagles, and ignoring him. 'Oh wow, an eagle. Great, but they are supposed to be here. What about me in this bleak and remote location. Didn't expect me to be here, did you, beardy?'

Delicate yet resilient, they are the most widespread bird in Britain, from lowland fens, to Highland moors. They are also Paul McCartney's favourite bird, apparently.

In ancient folklore, the wren hid among the feathers on the back of the eagle, and thus managed to fly higher, earning the name, cheekily, of King of All Birds.

All hail to the King!

Bonus Fact The wren is the only bird to feature on UK coins. From 1937, it appeared on the reverse of the farthing, a pre-decimal coin worth a quarter of a penny (about 2p in today's money). I used one as a plectrum to play my guitar (a farthing, not a wren).

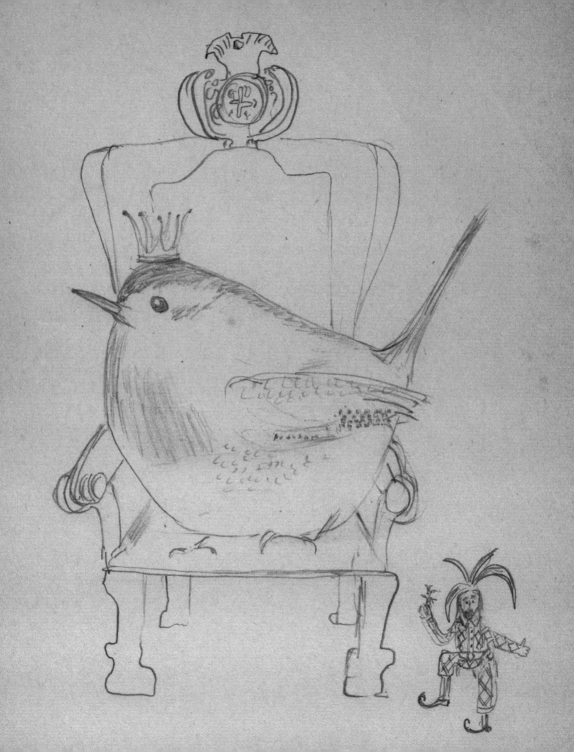

The Great Wren-Swan Tug Of War.

ROBIN.

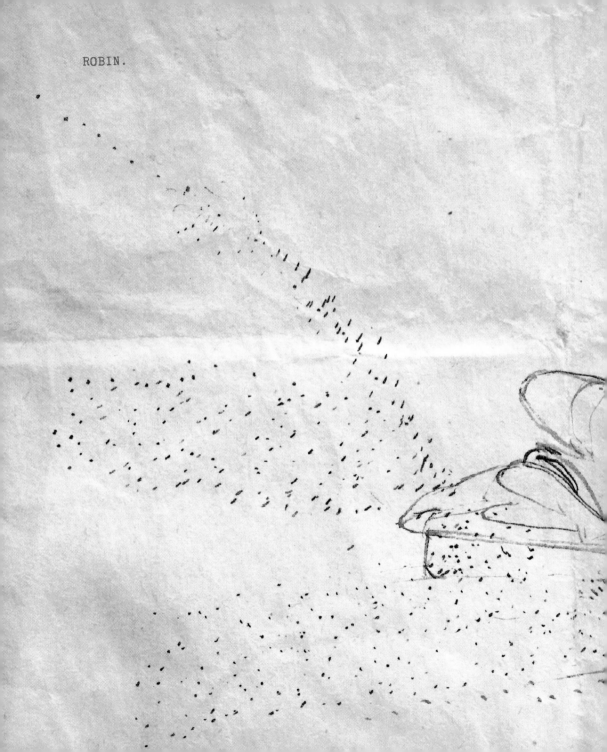

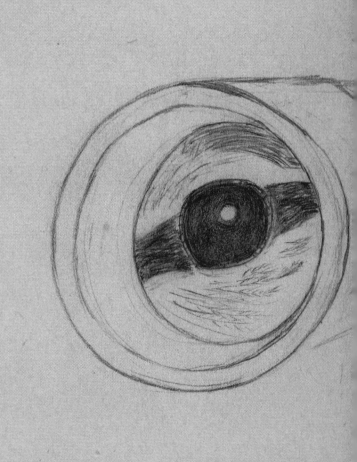

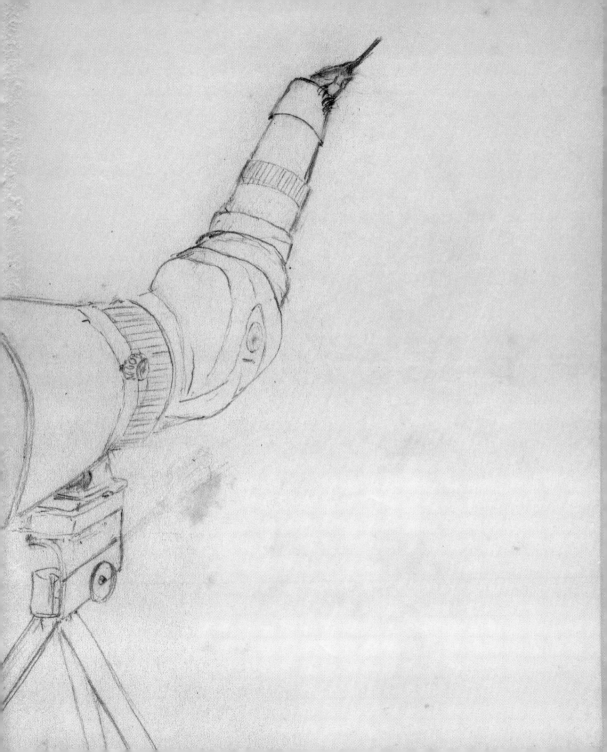

About the Author

Bill Bailey is a comedian, musician, actor and presenter. He is perhaps most well-known for his live shows - most recently Limboland, Qualmpeddler and The Remarkable Guide to the Orchestra. His work on television includes programmes such as Never Mind the Buzzcocks, Black Books and QI. He was also the host of Bill Bailey's Birdwatching Bonanza in January 2010, and wrote and presented his award-winning documentary about Alfred Russel Wallace, Bill Bailey's Jungle Hero, in 2013. He lives in west London with a small menagerie of animals and humans.

Acknowledgements

I'd like to thank my editor Katy Follain for all her
very helpful notes and suggestions, and the rest of the
excellent team at Quercus.
Also, I'd like to thank Susan, Luke, Neil, Liz, James,
Mita, Tash - the ace Glassbox team.
Thanks to my father, Christopher, for some great advice
and encouraging words.
Dax, for his astute critiques
and Sylvie for her great design suggestions.
Nick Blackbeard for some invaluable feedback.
To Joe for his visual wit and design brilliance.
And to my wife, Kris, whose good humour, encouragement
and unfailing support have kept me on track throughout
this entire project.

If you would like to help protect or even save birds, or would simply like more information, please go to The Royal Society for the Protection of Birds (rspb.org.uk), the British Trust for Ornithology (bto.org), the Wildfowl and Wetland Trust (wwt.org.uk), the International Centre for the Birds of Prey (icbp.org) and the Barn Owl Trust (barnowltrust.org.uk).

First published in Great Britain in 2016 by

Quercus Editions Ltd
Carmelite House
50 Victoria Embankment
London EC4Y 0DZ

An Hachette UK company

Illustrations by Bill Bailey
Design by Joe Magee www.periphery.co.uk
Internal photographs used under licence from Shutterstock.com

A CIP catalogue record for this book is available from the British Library

HB ISBN 978 1 78648 376 8

10 9 8 7 6 5 4 3 2 1

Printed and bound in Italy by L.E.G.O. S.p.A.